Secrets of
LOCAL ANESTHESIA and EXODONTIA

DR. SANDEEP KUMAR SHARMA   **DR. NIDHI SHARMA**   **DR. SHISHIR MOHAN**

© Dr. Sandeep Kumar Sharma,
Dr. Nidhi Sharma and Dr. Shishir Mohan 2023

All rights reserved

All rights reserved by author. No part of this publication may be reproduced, stored in a retrieval system or transmitted in any form or by any means, electronic, mechanical, photocopying, recording or otherwise, without the prior permission of the author.

Although every precaution has been taken to verify the accuracy of the information contained herein, the author and publisher assume no responsibility for any errors or omissions. No liability is assumed for damages that may result from the use of information contained within.

First Published in April 2023

ISBN: 978-93-5704-171-3

BLUEROSE PUBLISHERS

www.BlueRoseONE.com
info@bluerosepublishers.com
+91 8882 898 898

Distributed by: BlueRose, Amazon, Flipkart

THIS BOOK IS DEDICATED

TO

MY PARENTS

Smt. ASHA SHARMA

Shri. ABHINANDAN SHARMA

&

MY SIBLINGS

Er. PRASHANT SHARMA

Dr. NIDHI SHARMA

Highlights Of The Book

❖ MCQ's compiled here cover the whole subject in a text book manner.

❖ Text is organised into the 3 major sections having chapter wise question and answers.

❖ Illustrations in the form of diagramatic representation, clinical photographs, sketches, and flowcharts are included for easier understanding.

❖ Easily readable, understandable and emphasizes on relevant topics for competitive exams and viva-voice.

Dr. Sandeep Kumar Sharma is a budding Oral and Maxillo-facial Surgeon of India. He has done his bachelor and Masters of Dental Surgery from the Govt. University. He is fellow in Head & Neck Surgical Oncology at Regional Cancer Centre Gwalior, Madhya Pradesh. He is fellow in Oral Implantology from Spain. He is a life member of association of oral and maxillofacial surgeons of India. He has done numerous publications in national & international journals. He has been awarded many times in state chapter , national & international conferences. He is awarded for Best PG student of the year 2022 in Asia. He is awarded with swatantrata sangram senani uttaradhikari sangathan in the year 2023. He has been awarded for providing free treatment services to the prisoners in the District Jail Mathura. He has been awarded for providing free treatment camps in various places. He worked as JR at Surya Hospital, Ghaziabad. He worked at cancer centre in Ramkrishna Mission Sevashrama (Charitable Hospital), Vrindavan , Uttar Pradesh . He is also associated with True Smile Trichology Centre ,Guawahati , Assam . He is the founder & director of the Abhiash Maxillofacial Cancer Hospital & Trauma Centre, Delhi (under construction). Presently he is working as a consultant in dept. of Head & Neck Surgery in various part of the country.

Dr. Nidhi sharma did her schooling from Army Public School in Arunachal Pradesh Kimin, then shifted to Kendriya Vidyalaya, Kimin, Arunachal Pradesh . She did her graduation in Bachelor Of Dental Surgery from Govt. University. She did her fellowship in oral implantology from Spain (Murcia).She worked as a trainee in the department of Oral Oncology at Dharamshila Narayana Superspeciality Hospital, New Delhi. She has been awarded many times in state chapter , national & international conferences. She has done numerous publications in national & international journals. She was involved with different types of ascendancy & enhancement courses in various field such as in CBCT, Laser in dentistry, Magnification in dentistry & on CAD CAM as well. She has been awarded for providing free treatment services in camps in Delhi NCR region. She is resident at Surya Hospital, Ghaziabad, Uttar Pradesh. She is also associated with Shringar Skin Care & Laser Centre, Prayagraj, Uttar Pradesh. Presently she is Practicing Oral Surgery in Delhi NCR region.

 Dr. Shishir Mohan is a well known Oral and Maxillofacial surgeon of Agra-Mathura region, having 21 years experience in academics and research, he was Co- Director Smile Train Mathura as his main interest is the field of cleft surgery he is a Co-applicant in 2 patents in the field of Maxillofacial Surgery, he has also designed a new surgical flap "Braj Flap" for closure of Oro-Nasal Fistulas and has numerous national and international publications.

Foreword

BY DR. SANDEEP KUMAR SHARMA

A good book is always welcome. Every year, although hundreds of new books on dental subjects flood the market , only a few are considered to be outstanding by the students. It is therefore heartening to go through this text on secrets of local anesthesia and exodontia and find that it makes the grade as far as the content is concerned.

Including all the aspects of local anesthesia and exodontia in one book and that too in a question and answer format is a daunting task.

Such a format , i believe would be of great benefit to the students and all readers and would help them to prepare for competitive exams, viva as well as gain in – depth knowledge to build a strong foundation in oral surgery.

I hope and wish that the book " secrets of local anesthesia & exodontia with a complete question and explanatory answer's will prove to be an essential component of every dental library and clinic and will be an all- time companion to the dental students and professionals.

Dr. Sandeep kumar sharma

M.D.S, FICOI, FHNO

Preface

Secrets of local anesthesia and exodontia is a clinically oriented, student friendly textbook of oral and maxillofacial surgery. It can be used by students in traditional, systemic, combined traditional / systemic and problem based curricula and will be particularly useful to students when lectures and practicals in oral surgery are minimal. This book is very good for students who are willing to appear and crake various competative exams like NEET MDS exam, Army exam, Senior Residentship , govt & private interview based vacancy & many more exams. This book eliminates phobia of dental students related to teeth extraction and its complications. Students can also confidently deal in various medical emergencies. Important questions and answer with their explanation and diagrams are given in the book. The sequence we have choosen to follow is local anesthesia , extraction of teeth & medical emergencies. The illustration & are original and vibrant , and many views are unique. They have been designed to deal with the issues that students find particularly difficult, and provide a conceptual framework for building further understanding. We have used standard colors throughout the book, except where indicated otherwise. We ensure students will enjoy reading this book.

-Author's

About The Author

Dr. Sandeep Kumar Sharma is a budding Oral and Maxillo-facial Surgeon of India. He has done his bachelor and Masters of Dental Surgery from the Govt. University. He is fellow in Head & Neck Surgical Oncology at Regional Cancer Centre Gwalior, Madhya Pradesh. He is fellow in Oral Implantology from Spain. He is a life member of association of oral and maxillofacial surgeons of India. He has done numerous publications in national & international journals. He has been awarded many times in state chapter, national & international conferences. He is awarded for Best PG student of the year 2022 in Asia. He is awarded with swatantrata sangram senani uttaradhikari sangathan in the year 2023. He has been awarded for providing free treatment services to the prisoners in the District Jail Mathura. He has been awarded for providing free treatment camps in various places. He worked as JR at Surya Hospital, Ghaziabad. He worked at cancer centre in Ramkrishna Mission Sevashrama (Charitable Hospital), Vrindavan, Uttar Pradesh. He is also associated with True Smile Trichology Centre, Guawahati, Assam. He is the founder & director of the Abhiash Maxillofacial Cancer Hospital & Trauma Centre, Delhi (under construction). Presently he is working as a consultant in dept. of Head & Neck Surgery in various part of the country.

Acknowledgement

As much as I'd just love to take all the credit for this book, there are a lot of people who had a hand in making this dream come to life.

Firstly I would like to thanks to my father Shri Abhinandan Sharma, mother Smt. Asha Sharma, brother Er. Prashant Sharma & sister Dr. Nidhi Sharma who gave me the encouragement i needed throughout this process.

My heartfelt gratitude goes out to you. After the completion of this project. I experience feeling of achievement & satisfaction. Looking back on the completion of my project report I realize how impossible it was for me succeed on our own. I consider ourselves fortunate enough to be in right place with right person. Thank you for all Dr. Neelima Tyagi.

To all my friends –Dr. Shweta Verma, Dr. Shivani Upadhyay, Dr. Ayushi Yadav, Dr. Shruti Singh, Dr. Rajeev Ranjan Singh, Dr. Kajol Singh Rajput, Dr. Sameeksha Bhardwaj, Dr. Kashmira Solanki, Dr. Rashmi Kiran, Dr. Sahil Thakur, Dr. Pratishtha agrawal, Dr. Devna Sharma, whose patience & guidance made this work possible. To my friends this would have been a much more difficult feet without you.

To my teacher, Dr. DeviCharan Shetty, Dr. Manesh Lahori, Dr.Manju Kumari, Dr. Ajit Bhalla, Dr. Mohan Shishir, Dr. Neha Srivastava. Thank you all for your unwavering support & for reminding me to take breaks & have fun when I' have been stressed out.

Writing a book is harder than i thought and more rewarding than i could have ever imagined. None of this would have been possible without you uncle & aunty (Mr. Padam Yadav & Mrs. Amita Yadav) you taught me discipline, taught love, manners, respect & so much more that has helped me succeed in life. I truly have no idea where I'd be if you people hadn't given me a roof over my head or become my father & mother figure whom i desperately needed at this age.

Finally to all those who have been a part of my this journey, whose name are not mentioned above, thank you for pushing and inspiring & encouraging me as well in so many ways.

Above all, I thank the Almighty God for showering me with his blessings and love, showing me the way and providing me the inspiration throughout my life.

Contents

Local Anesthesia

    Types of local anesthetic injections are: 2

    Intraligamentary Technique 3

    How To Induce Local Anesthesia? 3

    Incisive Nerve Block Or Nasopalatine Nerve Block 6

    Infraorbital Nerve Block : 15

    Posterior Superior Alveolar Nerve Block 23

    Greater Palatine Nerve Block 29

    A. Mandibular Nerve Block With Closed –Mouth Technique 39

    B. Mandibular Nerve Block With Gow-Gates Technique 42

    Lingual Nerve Block 51

    Buccal Nerve Block 54

    Mental Nerve Block 57

    Incisive Nerve Block 60

Exodontia

    Introduction: 66

    Factors Complicating Dental Extraction 66

    Indications 66

    Contraindications 67

    Pre-Operative Assessment 68

    Principles Of Extraction 69

    Importance For Preoperative Radiographs 71

    Radiographic Requirements Of Pre Extraction 71

    Intra Alveolar Extraction 81

    The Correct Way Of Forceps Application 87

    Errors Encountered During Forcep Extraction 88

    Trans Alveolar Extraction 97

Shape Of Flaps 98

Laser For Extraction Of Impacted Teeth 106

Complications

Complications & Emergencies On Extraction Of Teeth 117

Recent Treatment Approach 129

Local Anesthesia

Defination: Local anesthesia is defined as a loss of sensation in a circumscribed area of the body caused by depression of excitation in nerve endings or an inhibition of the conduction process in peripheral nerves – Stanley F. Malamed

Types of local anesthetic injections are:-

1.) Local Infiltration

2.) Field Block

3.) Nerve Block

Local Infiltration:-

Small terminal nerve ending is the target site where local anesthetic is to be deposited preventing stimulation and creating of impulse.

Example :- In the interdental papillae in the anterior teeth region before incisive nerve block.

Field Block:-

Larger terminal nerve branches is the target site where local anesthetic is to be deposited. It prevents the nerve impulses reaching CNS from tissue.

Example:- above the apex of the teeth/tooth to be extracted.

Nerve Block:-

It is the main nerve trunk close to which local anesthetic solution is to be deposited.

Example :- Incisive Nerve Block.

NOTE :- In Dentistry, local infiltration is a type of field block.

Reason:- While infiltrating, it anesthetise the pulp and soft tissue around the injection site.

Let's Revise (MCQS)

Question- To give field block where should the Local Anesthesia be deposited ?

    a) Periodontal ligament

    b) Large branch of peripheral nerve

    b) Small nerve endings

    c) Main trunk.

Answer- b

Question- Which exemplifies a local infiltration ?

    a) Local anesthetic is deposited above the apex. Of a tooth before crown preparation.

    b) Local anesthetic is deposited near the main trunk for quadrant extraction.

    b) Local anesthetic is deposited in the interdental papillae to place a matrix band.

    c) Local anesthetic is deposited at the apex of tooth before restorative treatment.

Answer-b

Reason :- Local infiltration are deposited directly in the tissue being manipulated, at the small terminal nerve ending.

Intraligamentary Technique

It is a type of infiltration technique in which the anesthetic solution is deposited into the periodontal membrane of teeth.

NOTE :-

- 27-30 G, 0.3-0.4 mm in diameter (needle diameter).
- Angulation of needle – 30-40^0 in respect to long axis of tooth.
- Depth of penetration 2-3mm in periodontal tissue amount of deposition 0.2 ml of Local anesthesia.
- Single rooted teeth should be anesthetized with two injection.
- Multirooted teeth with one injection per root time 20 sec, whereas every following injection for the same tooth should last few seconds longer.

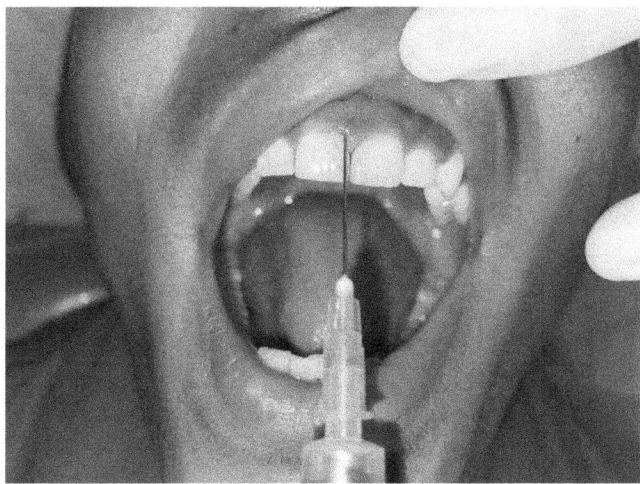

Topical Anesthesis:- Topical analgesia renders the free nerve endings in accessible structures.

Example :- abraded skin, cornes, mucous membrane.

How To Induce Local Anesthesia?

Depending upon the circumstances we choose the method among local infiltration, nerve block and field block. In dentistry the most commonly used routes is intra-oral technique. However, extra-oral technique is also used according to the indication.

Field block and local infiltration is further classified into various categories, they are :-

1.) Submucosal injection

2.) Intraosseous injection

3.) Interseptal injection

4.) Intraligamentary injection

1.> Submucosal injection :-

Path of penetration needle is inserted beneath the mucosal layers. Needle should come in contact with periosteum solution should move into cortex bone & in periosteum.

Note :- The term paraperiosteal is used in place of supraperiosteal because the solution do not go above but instead is deposited beside the periosteum.

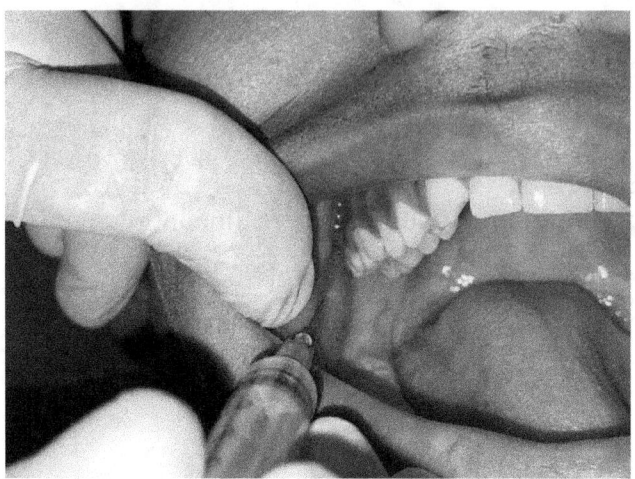

2.> Paraperiosteal Injection :-

Also known as Supraperiosteal injection or local infiltration. This technique is mainly used to achieve Pulpal anesthesia but the main disadvantage of this technique is, it needs multiple needle puncture to obtain anesthesia thus it leads systemic and local complication because a larger volume of anesthesia is used.

Nerve Anesthetized :- Large terminal branches of the dental plexus.

Area Anesthetized :-

- Branches of plexus.
- Tooth.
- Buccal Periosteum.
- Connective tissue.
- Mucous membrane.

Indication:-

- Pulpal anesthesia.
- Soft tissue anesthesia in a circumscribed area for surgical procedure.
- Primary molars.
- Hemostasis.

Contraindication :-
- Presence of infection or acute inflammation in the area of infection.
- Where there is dense bone.

Advantages :-
- Atraumatic procedure.
- Easy to induce.
- More success rate.
- It does not numb the tongue & lips.
- Shorter anesthetic duration.

Disadvantages :-
- Multiple needle insertions.
- Only recommended for smaller area.
- Larger volume of administration of LA solution.

Percent of positive aspiration :- Less than 1%.

Alternatives :- Regional Nerve Block, Periodontal ligament, Infra orbital.

Amount of solution deposit :- 0.6-1 ml

Target area :- Apex of tooth.

Needle insertion :- Mucobuccal fold.

Landmarks :-
- Mucobuccal fold.
- Long axis of tooth.

Recommended Needle :- 27 guage, short needle.

Orientation of bevel :- Toward bone

Clean the area
↓ (Using topical antiseptic)
Topical Anesthesia
↓
Stretch the tissue
↓
Insert the needle parallel to the long axis and above the apex of the root
↓
After achieving negative aspiration, inject 0.6 ml of solution for 20 second
↓
Wait for 3-5 minute

Signs & Symptoms :-
- No pain.
- No response with the use of EPT (Electric Pulp Testing).
- Feeling of numbers in the target site.

Failure of Anesthesia :-
- Needle too far from bone.
- Inadequate needle penetration (not adjacent to tooth apex).

Safety Measure :-
- Minimum risk of IV administration.
- Slow injection.

Complications :-

If the tip of needle is on the periosteum, it cause pain.

Incisive Nerve Block Or Nasopalatine Nerve Block

The other commonly used name is sphenopalatine nerve block or nervus incisivus.

Question -Why it is called sphenopalatine nerve block?

Answer -

Nasopalatine nerve, is the maxillary branch of trigeminal nerve, it is a sensory nerve. It courses into the nasal cavity through pterygopalatine ganglion to enter the sphenopalatine foramen.

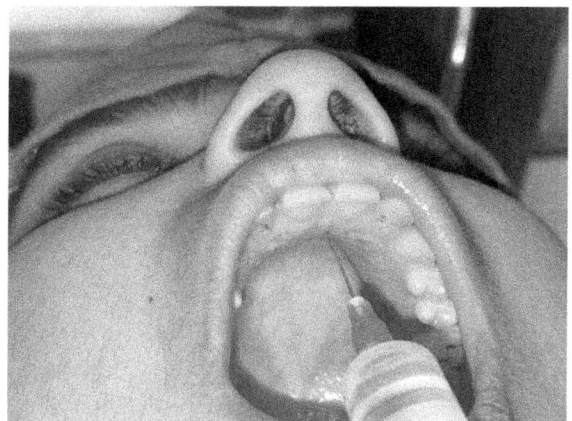

It is the most painful injection technique.

Two approaches of this block is :

1) Direct needle penetration lateral to the incisive papilla.
2) First anesthetized the interproximal papillae on the labial aspect between two central incisor than incisive foramen.

Question - Why second approach is important or why it need ?

Answer- Because it is less traumatic and less painful than direct one puncture technique. By doing this the labial interdental papillae get easily anesthetized, and the circumscribed area get anesthetized, patient will not feel any sensation after that.

Amount of solution deposit :-

- By 1st approach – 0.25 to 0.5 ml into incisive canal.
- By 2nd approach – 0.25 ml to 0.3 ml in labial papillae.

    (multiple penetration) – 0.3 ml to 0.5 ml into the incisive canal.

Target area :- Incisive foramen

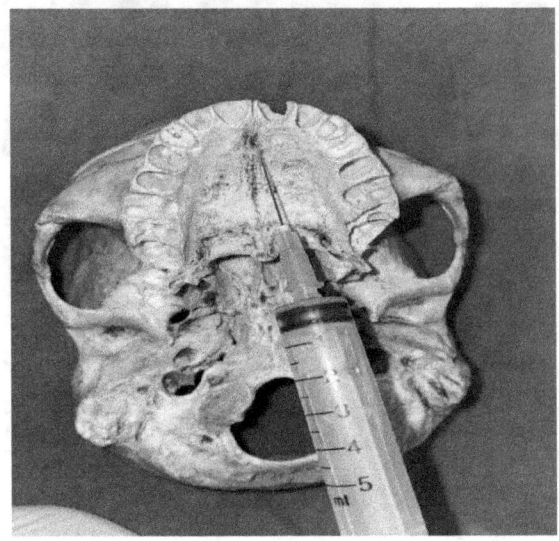

Question - How would we know where is incisive foramen ?

Answer - 0.5 cm beyond the central incisor in a straight line.

Nerve Anesthetized :- Nasopalatine nerve and left side.

Area Anesthetized :-

- Labial and lingual interdental papillae of anterior region bilaterally.
- Anterior portion of hard palate and the soft tissue overlying it.
- Bilaterally first premolar till the mesial aspect.

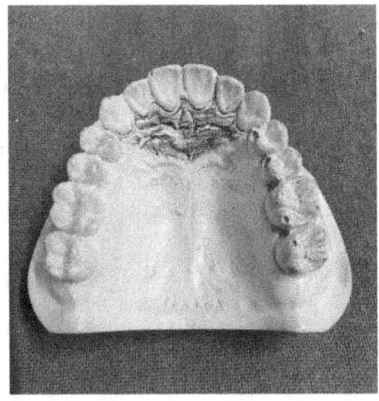

Indication :-

- For extraction of upper six anterior teeth.
- To anesthetize the anterior hard palate.
- Soft tissue surgery of anterior region in labial and lingual surface.
- To anesthetize nasal septum.
- To supplement middle & anterior superior alveolar nerve block.

Contraindication :-

- Infection and inflammation on the target site.

Advantages :-

- ✓ Requires less volume of solution.
- ✓ Pain regresses on using multiple needle penetration technique.

Disadvantages :-

- Difficult to stabilize the needle.
- Painful injection technique so patient feels more discomfort.
- No hemostasis except in the immediate area of injection.
- Need more force to deposit the solution (sometime it flush back if needle hub is not stabilized properly.
- Usually within the patient's sight while injecting from front.

MCQ :- An infection may trail a nasopalatine nerve block, in which scenario?

a) The needle tip is inserted directly into the incisive papilla.

b) The anesthetic solution is deposited too quickly.

c) The needle is inadvertently advanced solution is exceeded.

d) Infection not possible at all

Answer - c

Explanation :- Infection may follow the nasopalatine nerve block, if the needle is inadvertently advanced into the incisive canal to enter the floor of the nose.

MCQ - Following the nasopalatine nerve block, dental treatment can begin within.

a) 1-2 minutes

b) 2-3 minutes

c) 3-4 minutes

d) 4-5 minutes

Answer -b

MCQ - Which sequence of injections leads to an atraumatic nasopalatine nerve block?

a) Labial frenum, incisive papilla, interproximal papilla.

b) Interproximal papilla, labial frenum, incisive papilla.

c) Incisive papilla, labial frenum, interproximal papilla.

d) Labial frenum, interproximal papilla, incisive papilla.

Answer -d

Explanation :- In the multiple injection technique, three injections are used to deliever atraumatic nasopalatine anesthesia, first, on infiltration of the labial frenum, followed by an injection directly into the interproximal papilla between the central incisors. The final injection is into the soft tissues lateral to the incisive papilla.

Question - Why this injection technique is more painful ?

Answer - When injecting the operator encounters significant resistance. To overcome this, one needs to apply more pressure on the plunger to deposit the solution. This results in the production of higher pressure within non-resilient tissues, leading to pain, ischemia & possible tissue damage.

Question - How to overcome the complan of pain ?

Answer - By using the insulin syringe and slow deposition by taking more time.

Question - What is the normal rate of deposition of solution ?

Answer - 1 ml / minute or 1.8 ml in 100 second.

Percentage of positive aspiration – less than 1 %.

Question - Why do we need to aspirate ?

Answer - The solution is not delivered into a blood vessel. Aspiration consists of drawing back on the plunger once the needle has been inserted to see if any blood enters into the syringe.

Question - What happens if the blood get mix with LA solution ?

Answer - The PH of both the solution get change & it will not show the adequate result.

Question - Should we continue the injection even if it get mix with blood ?

Answer - No, ideally it should be discarded.

MCQ - Which of the following statement's regarding the action of local anesthetics is true?

    a) There is little relation between H ion concentration & anesthetic activity.

    b) Less the PH of in an area, less effective is the action of an anesthetic agent.

    c) There is no relation between H ion concentration and anesthetic activity.

    d) More the PH in an area less effective is the action of anesthetic agent.

Question - What is the ideal time to aspirate ?

Answer - 2-3 second.

<u>Alternative</u> :-
- Local infiltration.
- Unilateral nerve block of maxilla.
- Unilateral anterior and middle superior alveolar nerve block.

<u>Amount of solution deposit</u> :- 0.25- 0.5 ml.

Target area :- Palatal mucosa just lateral to the incisive papilla.

Needle insertion :- 0.5 cm beyond palatal aspect of maxillary central incisor.

Landmarks :-

- Bilateral Central Incisor.
- Incisive Papilla in the palatal midline.

Recommended Needle :- 25 guage needle or 27 guage needle.

Orientation of bevel :- Towards palatal soft tissue.

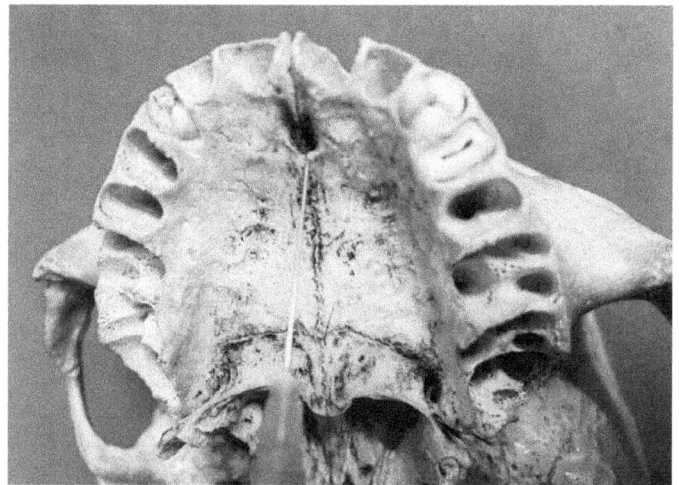

Question - Why the orientation of bevel is towards bone ?

Answer - To be guided directly to the target area without deviation?

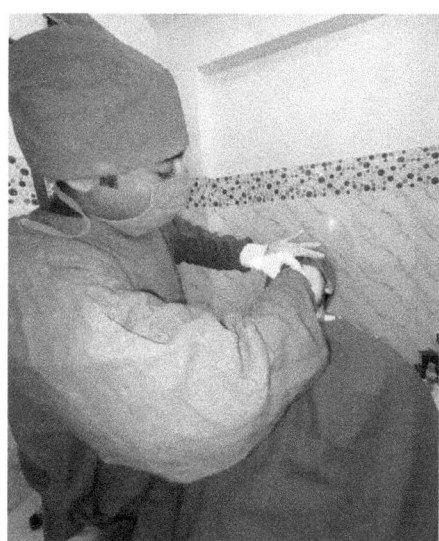

Operator Position :- 9 or 10 'o clock position.

Procedure

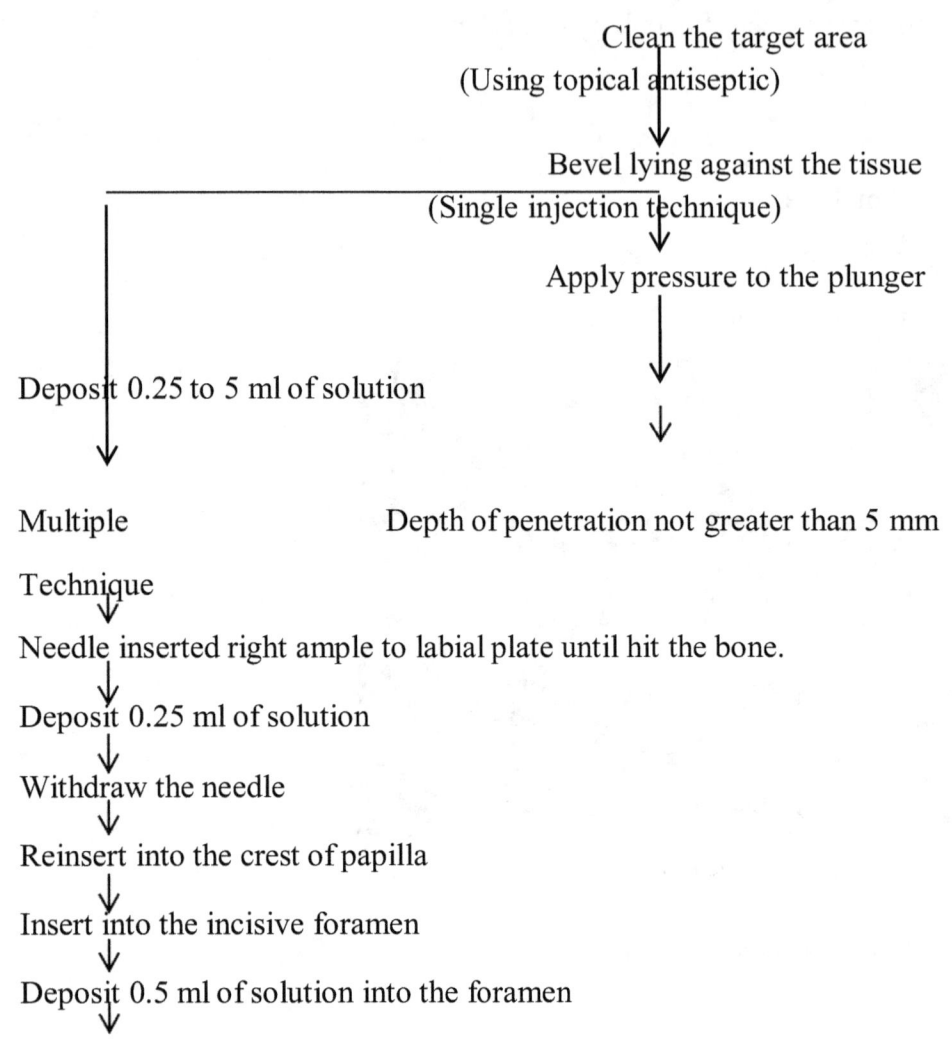

A
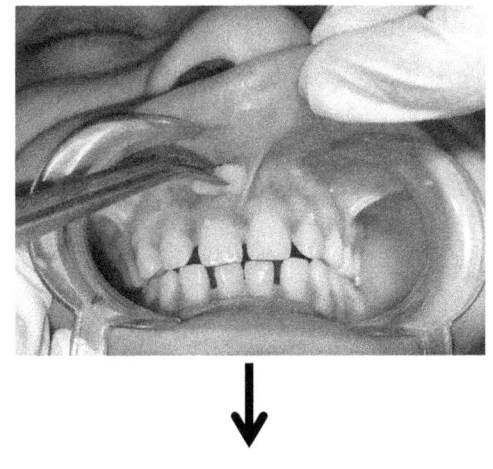

B
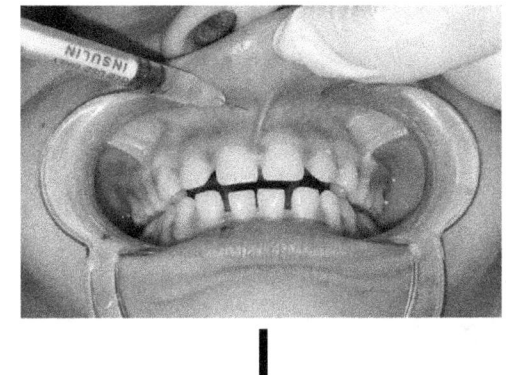

C
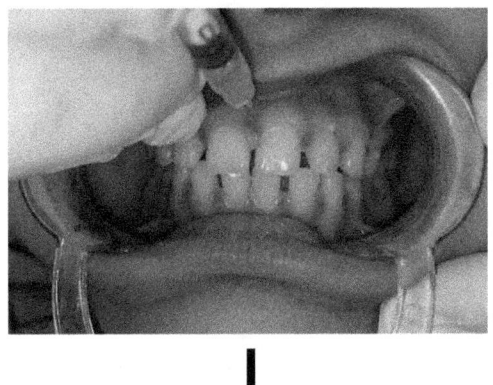

D
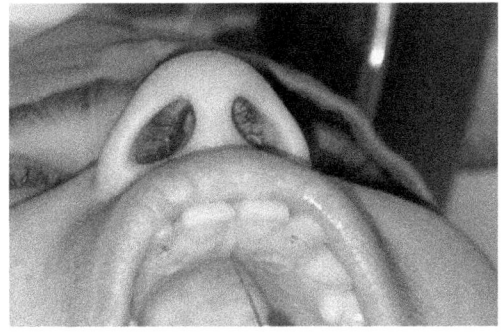

Sign & Symptoms :- Objective & subjective
- Absence of pain with the instrument.
- Numbness in the palate while touching with tongue.
- Numbness of upper lip bilaterally

Failure of anesthesia :-
- Success rate is more than 95 %.
- Inadequate deposition of solution.
- Inadequate needle penetration.

Safety Measures :-
- Aspiration
- Contact with bone

Complications :-
- When using high concentrated vasoconstrictor, it will necrose the soft tissue.

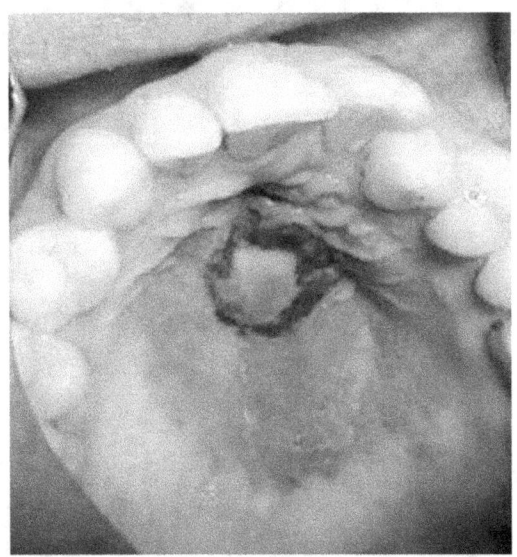

- Flush back of the solution.
- Breakage of needle on forceful application or banding of needle.

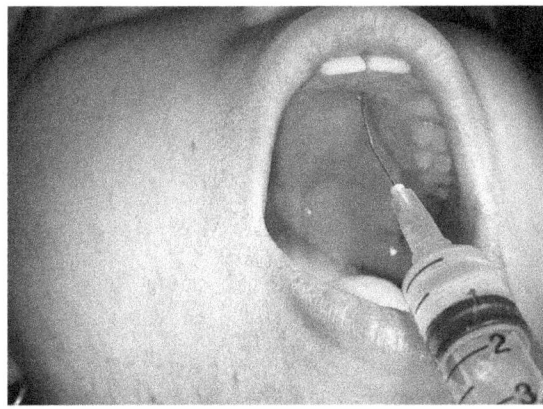

Question - Why does the solution flush back ?

Answer - It is because the hub of the syringe loosens up while applying more pressure or force to deposit the solution in the target area.

Infraorbital Nerve Block :-

The other name for this block is Middle Superior Alveolar and Anterior Superior Alveolar Nerve Block.

Question - Why this name is given for this block ?

Answer - Because Middle Superior Alveolar and Anterior Superior Alveolar is the branch of the Infra-orbital nerve, so while injecting in Infra-orbital foramen to block Infra-orbital Nerve, this two terminal branches also get anesthetize.

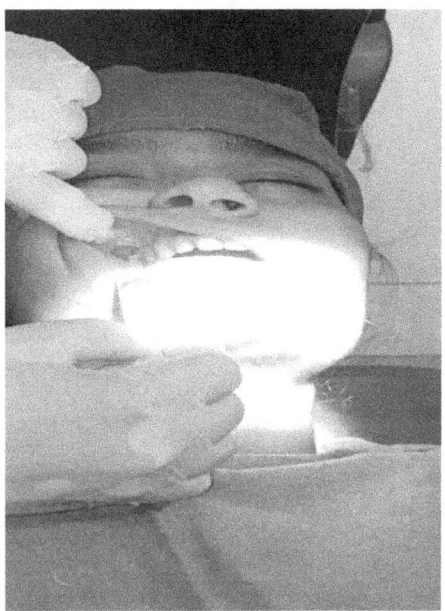

Amount of solution deposited :- 0.9 -2 ml of solution.

Target area :- Infraorbital foramen.

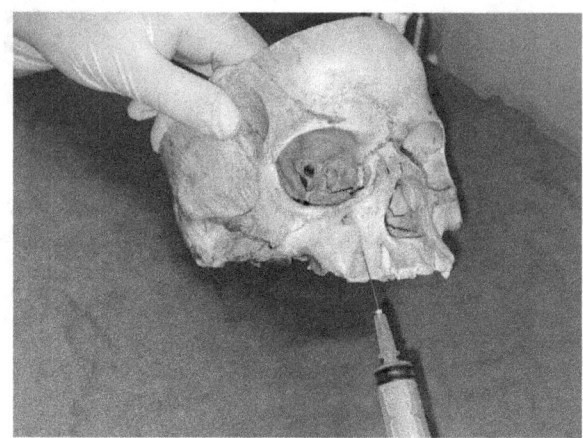

Position of needle between maxillary premolars for a middle superior alveolar nerve block.

Question - Where is Infraorbital foramen located ?

Answer - Infraorbital foramen is located in Infra-orbital depression which is located in a line parallel to the long axis of second bicuspid tooth bilaterally.

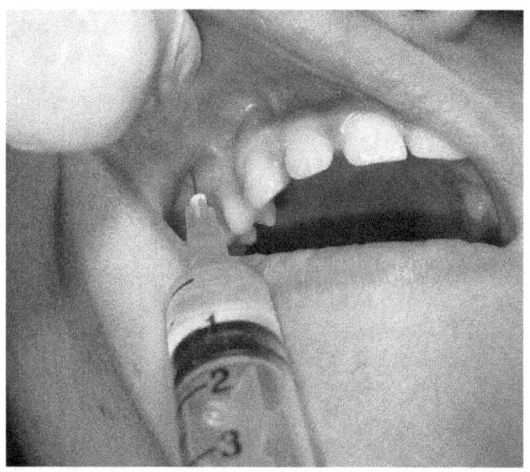

Nerve Anesthetized :-

Infra-orbital Nerve (Middle Superior Alveolar Nerve and Anterior Superior Alveolar Nerve) other terminal branches like superior labial nerve (which supply the upper lip), Lateral Nasal (Which supplies the lateral side of nose) and Inferior palpebral (which supplies lower eyelids).

Area Anesthetized :-

- All three anterior teeth of the same side.
- Both bicuspid teeth of the same side & mesiobuccal root of first molar on injected side, Zygomatic buttress, side of the nose, Alveolar bone and portion of Zygomatic bone. Soft tissue like – lower eyelids, upper lip, Alar part of nose & depressor septi.

Indication :-

- When it is needed to block the middle & Anterior Superior Alveolar Nerve Block.
- Any operative procedure in the five teeth of same side.
- When ASA block fail to anesthetize.

- Wound closure.

Contraindication :-

- Infection or inflammation in the target area.
- In general anesthesia.
- Distortion of anatomic landmarks.
- Any allergy or sensitivity to the anesthetic agent.
- Uncooperative patient.

Advantages :-

- Requires less anesthetic medication to produce desired effect.
- Requires single penetration to inject the solution.

Disadvantages :- None.

Question - What if the patient is un cooperative ?

Answer - Plan under sedation or General anesthesia.

Percent of positive aspiration :- less than 3 %

Alternatives :-

- Local infiltration.
- Anterior Superior Alveolar Nerve Block.

Needle Insertion :- 5 mm from mucobuccal fold in a line parallel to pupil of eye, supra & infra orbital notch, infra-orbital foramen & mental foramen.

Landmarks :- Infra orbital ridge, Infra orbital depression, Supraorbital notch & Infraorbital notch, anterior teeth & Pupil of the eye.

Recommended Needle :- 25 or 27 guage needle.

Orientation bevel :- Towards bone.

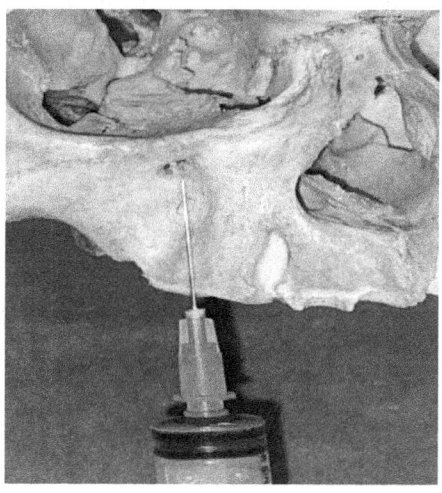

Operator position :- 10 o'clock position.

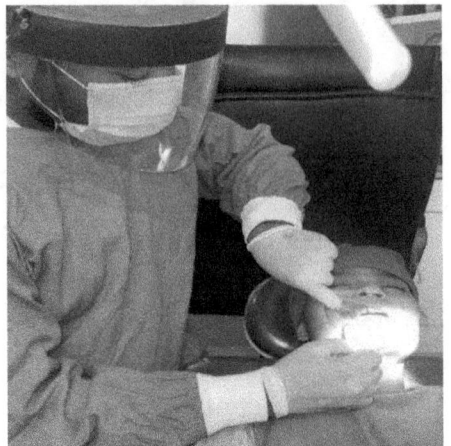

Procedure :-

Maxillary occlusal plan making 45⁰ angle to the floor.
↓
Clean the target area
↓ (Using topical antiseptic)
Apply topical anesthesia above maxillary canine
↓
Find the infra orbital foramen by moving finger tip 0.5 cm downward to the infra orbital notch.
↓
Retract the upper lip with non- injecting hand
↓   ↓   ↓
Needle directed superiorly and   Bisect the crown of central incisor
of Remain parallel to second premolar until   the operating area into mesial and
It is palpated near foramen   distal half

Run the needle diagonally bisecting   ↓

mesioincisal and distogingival angle
↓
Deposit the solution keeping in mind

It should touch the foramen boundaries
↓
Insert no more than 3/4th needle

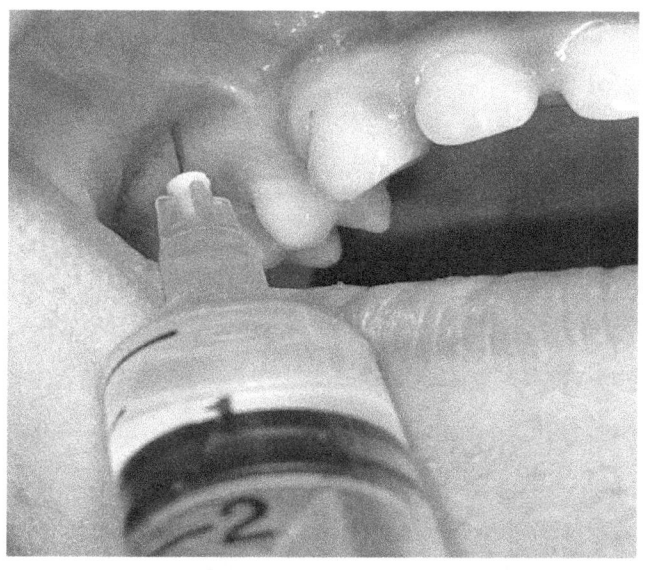

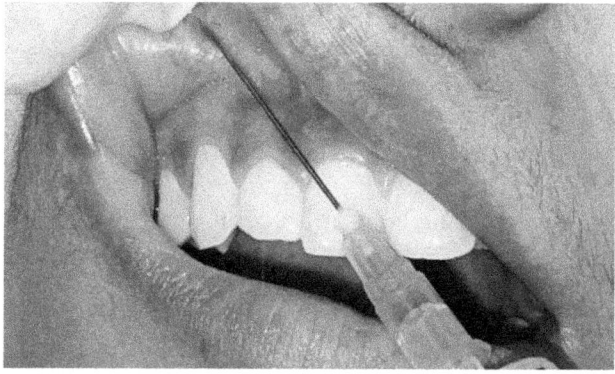

Question - Why is it indicated to insert the needle not more than 3/4th of its length ?

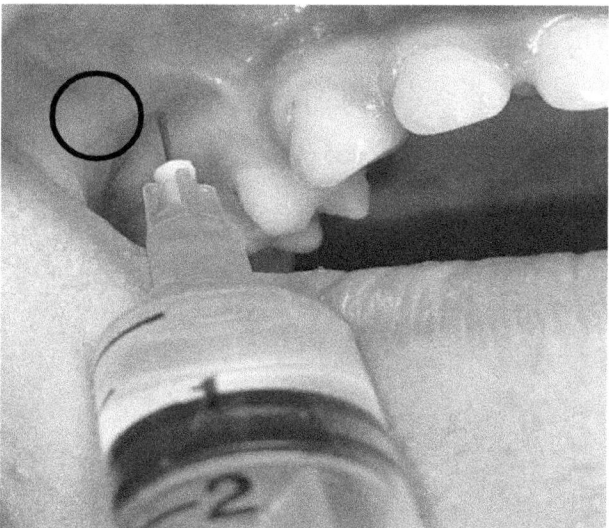

Answer - In case if the needle breaks, it should be visualized in the oral cavity so that by holding 1/4th of the end of needle one can remove the broken needle easily or else it will go for operative procedure.

Sign & Symptoms :-

- Absence of pain with instrumentation.

- Tingling and numbness over zygoma, lower eyelid, upper lip, side of the nose.
- No response with the use of EPT.

<u>Failure Of Anesthesia :-</u>

With or without dental anesthesia the patient can feel anesthesia of upper lip, side of nose, below eyelid.

<u>Reason Being:-</u>

ASA do not anesthetized properly.

Question - What can one do to anesthetize the area ?

Answer - Give the Supraperiosteal injection over first premolar.

<u>Complication</u> :- Hematoid, bleeding, infection, blood vessel, injury, unintentional injection of anesthetic into blood vessel, nerve damage of edema allergic reaction to anesthetic medication.

Question - How can one manage Hematoma formation ?

Answer - Due to injury to the wall of a blood vessel, promoting blood to seep out of the blood vessel into the surrounding tissues an injury to any type of blood vessel (artery, vein, capillary) cause hematoma formation.

One should also know the extra-oral approach for infra orbital nerve block.

<u>Procedure</u>

Clean the infra orbital region extraorally using an antiseptic solution
↓
palpate inferior border on the infra orbital rim.
↓
Insert needle through skin, subcutaneous tissue & muscle. Before injecting the anesthetic, aspirate to ensure the needle is not within the vessel. Inject the antiseptic.
↓
Use 1 ½ inch, 25 gauge needle. Direction of needle upward & medially do not exceed the depth of 1/8 inch.

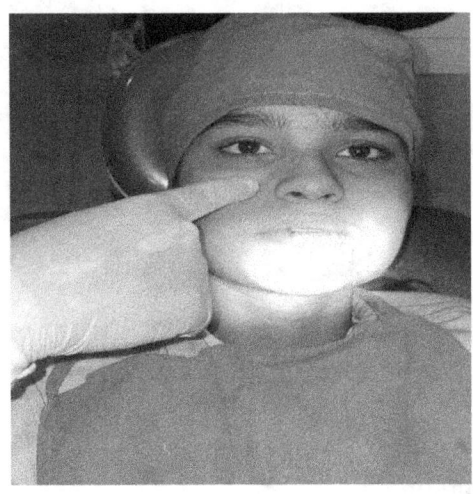

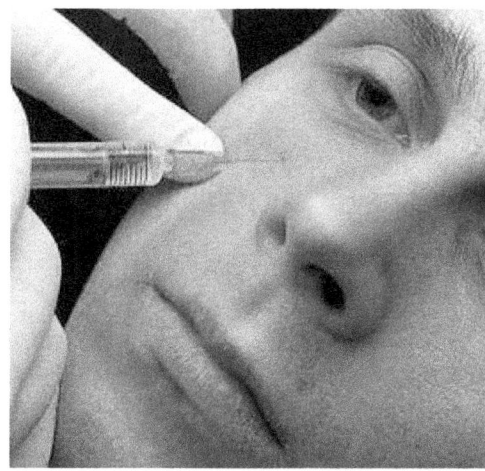

NOTE :- Due to proximity of facial nerve when the extraoral approach is used, it is best to use an anesthetic agent that does not contain added medication with vasoconstrictor properties. The overlying tissue should appear edematous massage for 10-15 second.

Question - When the extra oral technique one can use ?

Answer - When intra orally it is not possible to anesthetize ASA & MAS because of trauma, infection or other reason. When intra oral method have been ineffective.

Landmarks :-

- Pupil of eye.
- Infraorbital ridge.
- Infraorbital notch
- Infraorbital depression.

NOTE :- Sometimes Posterior Superior alveolar nerve is also anesthetized.

MCQS-The Middle Superior Alveolar (MSA) nerve is presence in which percentage of people.

   a) 8%

   b) 28%

   c) 78%

   d) 98%

Answer- b

Explanation :- The anterior superior alveolar nerve usually provides premolar innervation for a majority of the population.

MCQS - The success rate of MSA nerve block is

   a) High

   b) Moderate

   c) Low

   d) Negligible

Answer- a

MCQS -Which penetration site correlates with the MSA nerve block?

a) Height of mucobuccal fold over maxillary first molar.

b) Height mucobuccal fold over maxillary second molar.

c) Height of mucobuccal fold over maxillary first premolar.

d) Height of mucobuccal fold over maxillary second premolar.

Answer- d

MCQS - The ASA nerve block will not anesthetize which?

a) Lower eyelid

b) Upper lip

c) Lateral aspect of nose

d) Anterior hard palate

Answer - d

Reason :- Anterior hard palate is anesthetized by the nasopalatine, not ASA nerve block.

MCQS - The administrator of an ASA nerve block should.

a) Feel the needle through the facial skin as it advances towards the target.

b) Feel the anesthetic solution as it is deposited.

c) See a visible swelling or ballooning of the tissues during anesthetic deposition.

d) See 4mm of needle when the correct depth of penetration is reached.

Answer - b

Explanation :- The administrator will feel the anesthetic through the finger over the infraorbital foramen, where the solution is being injected & 16 not 4 mm of long needle is usually visible at the correct depth of penetration use of a short needle is not recommended for the ASA block. The needle should not be palpable through the skin (The needle should be redirected if its path is too superficial). If the needle tip is at infraorbital foramen, swelling or ballooning of the tissues during deposition of ASA nerve block should not occur.

MCQS - Which is recommended for ASA nerve block?

a) Pressure syringe.

b) Computer controlled local anesthetic delivery (C-CLAD).

c) Conventional self – aspirating syringe.

d) Jet injector (needless syringe)

Answer - b

Reason :- A conventional self – aspirating syringe can safely deliever the AMSA block, but a C-CLAD is recommended because it improves the ease and comfort of the injection.

Posterior Superior Alveolar Nerve Block

Posterior Superior Alveolar Nerve Block is also known as tuberosity block or Zygomatic block.

Question - Why PSA nerve block is called tuberosity block?

Answer - PSA nerve block is called Tuberosity block because while injecting, the path of insertion is located Posterosuperior and medial to the maxillary tuberosity.

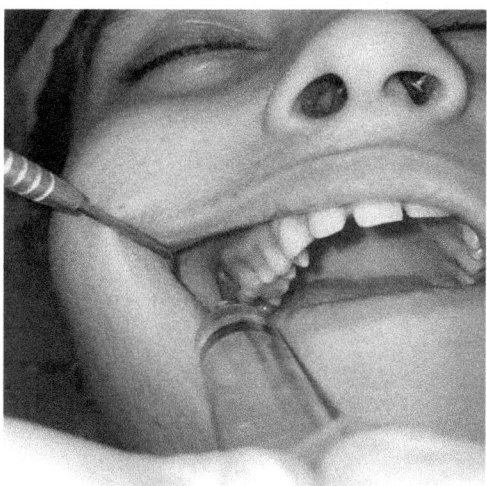

Nerves Anesthetized :- Posterior Superior Alveolar Nerve

Area Anesthetized :- It anesthetizes Pulp of Maxillary molars.

- Buccal alveolar process of maxillary molars.
- Periosteum.
- Mucous membrane
- Connective tissue Overlying these teeth

Note :- PSA does not anesthetize mesiobuccal root of first molar and it is anesthetize by middle superior alveolar block.

Only 2 % success rate.

Indication :-

- For surgical procedure or extraction of molars and supporting structures.
- When supraperiosteal injection has failed to anesthetize the area.
- When supraperiosteal injection is contraindicated.

Contraindication :-

- When there is chances of haemorrhage.
- Patient on a drug that increases bleeding (eg – Coumadin/ clopidogrel).
- Hemophilic patient.

Question - Why is PSA along with extra nerve blocks is contraindicated in Hemophilia ?

Answer - PSA is contraindicated is Hemophilia because there is deficiency of one or more cloting factors and this leads to prolonged clotting time & excessive bleeding tendencies. Deficient factors are factor VII,IX,XI.

Advantages :-

- Success rate is more, greater than 95 %.
- Only single penetration is needed to anesthetize.
- Atraumatic (because of large tissue space available to accommodate the anesthetic solution & fact that bone is not touched.
- Minimizes total volume of anesthetic solution.
- Comfortable for the patient.

Disadvantages :-

- When working on First molar, second injection is necessary that is MSA.
- Difficult to locate the target area.
- Chances of hematoma formation.

Question - Why is it difficult to locate the target area while injecting ?

Answer - It is difficult because there is no bony landmarks and reliable on soft tissue only. Percentage of positive aspiration :- 3.1 %

Alternatives :-

- Maxillary Nerve Block.
- Supraperiosteal or PDL injections.
- Local infiltration.

Amount of solution deposit :- 0.9 – 1.8 ml of anesthetic solution.

Target area :- Height of muccobuccal fold over second molar.

Needle insertion:-

Children :- 10 -14 mm

In adult :- 16 mm

With using long needle – inserted half its length.

With using short needle – approximate 4mm should remain visible.

Needle penetrates the mucosa areolar tissue, and possibly the buccal pad of fat. It penetrate the Posterior fibers of buccinators muscle.

Recommended Needle:- Short needle, 25/27 guage.

Orientation of bevel :- Towards bone during injection.

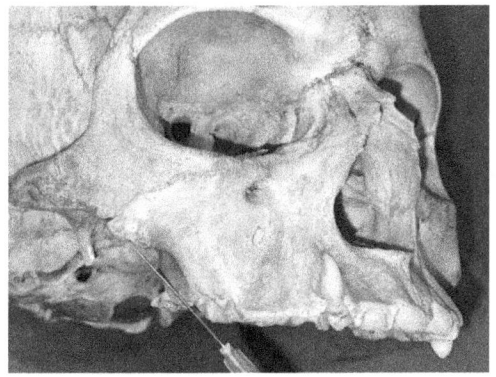

Operator position :- 10 or 8 o'clock position.

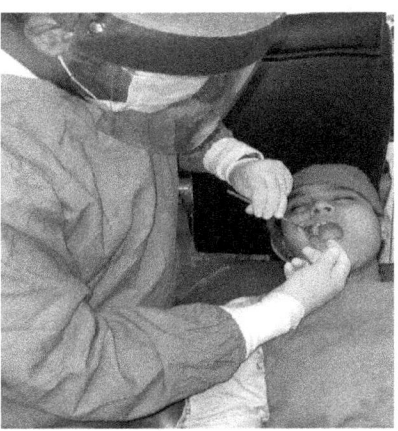

Procedure :-

Clean the target area
↓
(Using topical antiseptic)

Bevel towards bone
↓
Move the finger tip along the Zygomatic process of maxilla posteriorly over the mucobuccal fold. Identify the concavity in the mucobuccal fold.
↓
Rotate your finger so that the bulbous portion is in contact with posterior surface of zygomatic process
↓
Pull the mandible to the side of injection.
↓
After retracting the cheek insert the needle into the height of mucobuccal fold over second molar in upward, inward & backward direction.
↓
(Do not hit the bone)

Insert around 16 mm of needle length or ½ - ¾ "th inch
↓
(Hold the needle in a pen grasp position)

After aspiration, deposit 0.9- 1.8 ml of solution over 30-60 sec.
↓
Withdraw the needle safely
↓
Wait & watch for 3-5 min for sign & symptoms.

Sign & Symptoms :-

- No subjective symptoms.
- Absence of pain during instrumentation & treatment.

Failure Of Anesthesia :-

- Needle too far posteriorly.
- Needle not high enough.
- Needle more medially or more laterally.
- Over insertion of needle.

Safety Measures :-

- Aspirate before injecting.
- Do not deposit the solution too fast.
- Careful observation because it relay on soft tissue.

Complications :-

- Hematoma.
- Hemorrhage.
- Mandibular Anesthesia.

Question - Why there is chances of mandibular anesthesia ?

Answer - Because mandibular division of trigeminal nerve is located lateral to PSA nerve. In case one deposited the local anesthetic solution more laterally it will anesthetize the mandibular branch.

Question - Why hematoma is common with PSA block ?

Answer - Because too far posteriorly into pterygoid plexus of veins. The maxillary artery may be perforated.

Question - How can one minimize hematoma formation ?

Answer - By using needle, because this minimize the risk of pterygoid plexus puncture.

MCQS - Of the following in which condition local anesthesia is ineffective.

a) Edema

b) Anemia

c) Localized infection

d) Hematoma

Answer- c

Explanation :- In infected area, a low tissue of PH is found. This will interfere with the development of anesthesia by preventing liberation of free base (RN).

MCQS - Most difficult maxillary tooth to anesthetize by infiltration is :

a) 1st molar

b) Canine

c) 3rd molar

d) 1st premolar

Answer - a

Explanation :- 1st maxillary molar is difficult to anesthetize because mesiobuccal root of 1st maxillary molar is not anesthetized by Posterior Superior Alveolar Nerve Block. It required additional nerve block i.e., Middle Superior Alveolar Nerve Block. So, basically to anesthetize single tooth we require two nerve block. (MSA & PSA).

MCQS - Hematoma is more frequent with?

a) Inferior nerve block

b) Greater Palatine nerve block

c) Posterio Superior Alveolar Nerve Block

d) Infra Orbital Nerve Block

Answer - c

Explanation :- Hematoma is most commonly associated with Posterior Superior Alveolar and infraorbital nerve block. Hematoma formation in Posterior Superior Alveolar Nerve Block is due to injury of Pterygoid Plexus of veins, which results in immediate swelling of face. To avoid this short needle are used.

MCQS - During Posterior Superior Alveolar nerve block, the anatomical landmark used are mucobuccal fold, occlusal plane, coronoid process & anterior border of :-

a) Premolar

b) Ramus

c) Mandible

d) Midline

Answer - b

MCQ - The needle is advanced in Posterior Superior Alveolar.

a) Downward, inward and forward direction.

b) Upward, outward & forward direction.

c) Upward, Inward, & backward direction.

d) Upward outward & backward direction.

Answer - c

Explanation :- In Posterior Superior Alveolar Nerve Block, needle is advanced slowly in upward, inward & backward direction in one movement.

- Upward – Superiorly at a 45 degree angle to the occlusal plane.
- Inward – medially towards the midline at a 45 degree angle to occlusal plane.
- Background – Posteriorly at 45 degree angle to the long axis of second molar.

MCQS - During Posterior Superior Alveolar Nerve Block which of the structure is pierced.

a) Buccinator

b) Lateral Pterygoid

c) Medial Pterygoid

d) Masseter

Answer - a

Explanation :- The needle Penetrates the mucosa, areolar tissue, and possibly the buccal pad of fat. It penetrates the Posterior fibres of buccinators muscles.

MCQS - The Posterior Superior Alveolar Nerve does not consistently innervate which root?

a) Palatal root of maxillary first molar

b) Mesiobuccal root of maxillary second molar

c) Distobuccal root of maxillary second molar

d) Mesiobuccal root of maxillary second molar

Answer - b

Explanation :- The position alveolar nerve does not always innervate the mesiobuccal root of the maxillary first molar, in same patient (28 %) the middle superior alveolar nerve innervates the root.

MCQS - Which needle is recommended for PSA block?

a) 25- guage short needle

b) 25- guage long needle

c) 27- guage short needle

d) 27- guage long needle

Answer - c

MCQS - Which is the correct penetration depth when administering a PSA block to a child?

a) 10 mm

b) 16 mm

c) 20 mm

d) 25 mm

Answer - a

Explanation :- The depth of penetration for PSA block depends on the size of the patient's skull. For most average adults the depth of penetration is 16 mm ; However, for individuals with smaller skulls, like children, the needle is halted at 10-14 mm.

MCQS - To safely administer the PSA nerve block.

a) Slowly deposit 1.8 ml over 20 to 30 seconds.

b) Aspirate in two planes, a several times during the anesthetic deposition.

c) Guide a long needle into the tissue until 4 mm of the shaft remains visible.

d) Advances the needle upward 4 mm, then inward 4mm, and finally backward 4mm.

Answer - b

Explanation :- Frequent multiplane aspirations before deposition and during the injection enhance the safety of PSA block.

MCQS - A needle – induced hematoma at the Pterygoid Plexus of veins.

a) Is visible intraorally within several seconds.

b) Is produced by inserting the needle too far laterally.

c) Is typically seen in the buccal tissues of mandibular region.

d) Is easily controlled when pressure is applied to injection site.

Answer - c

Explanation :- A needle – induced hematoma at the Pterygoid Plexus of veins in the buccal tissues of mandibular region.

Greater Palatine Nerve Block

Greater Palatine nerve block is also known as Anterior Palatine nerve block.

Question - Greater Palatine nerve is a branch of which major nerve and from where Greater Palatine nerve emerges ?

Answer - Greater Palatine nerve is a branch of maxillary nerve which is a divison of trigeminal nerve. Maxillary Nerve emerges from foramen rotendum and Greater Palatine nerve emerges from Greater Palatine foramen.

Amount of solution deposited :- 0.25 ml to 0.6 ml.

Target area :- Greater Palatine Foramen.

Question - Where does Greater Palatine foramen located ?

Answer - On average Greater Palatine Foramen is located.

15.9 ± 1.5 mm from midline maxillary suture.

3.0 ± 1.2 mm from alveolar ridge.

17.0 ± 1.5 mm from Posterior nasal

spine. Or

Between the second and third maxillary molars about 1 cm toward the midline of the palate from palatal gingival margin.

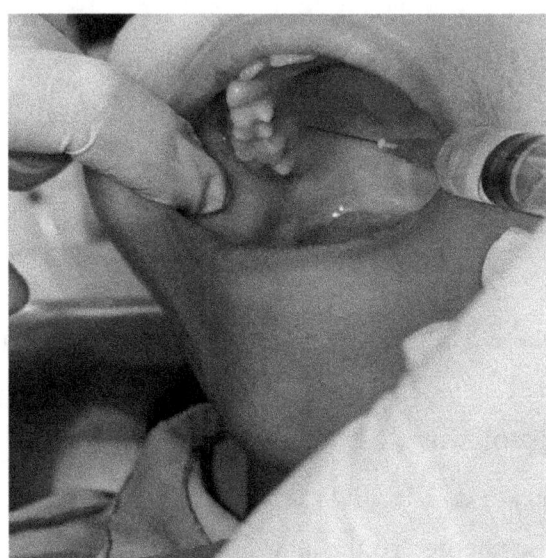

Intresting Fact :-

Greater Palatine nerve block was first discovered in the year 1927 by Matsuda.

Nerve anesthetized :- Anterior Palatine Nerve

Area anesthetized :-

- Midline of hard and Soft Palate.
- Premolars and molars teeth.
- Posterior portion of hard and soft palate

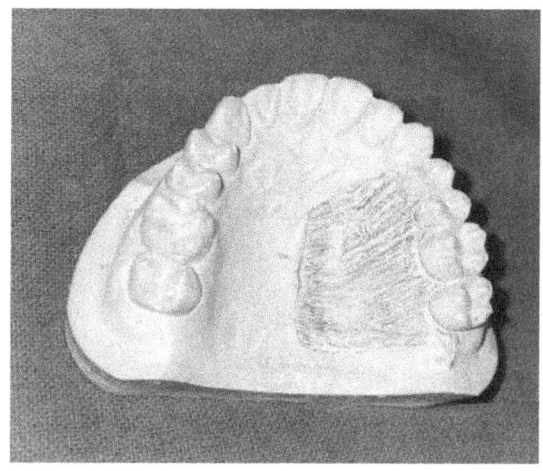

Note :- Some author believe this also anesthetized the wall of maxillary sinus. Indications :-

- To control the pain during any surgical procedure on hard and soft palatal tissue.
- Sub gingival restoration of posterior teeth.
- Extraction of posterior teeth.

Contraindications :-

- Any inflammation or infection in the area of injection site.
- Needed to work in small area.

Advantages :-

- Requires single needle penetration to anesthetize.
- Reduce patient discomfort.
- Need smaller volume of anesthetic solution.

Disadvantages :-

- A liitle traumatic while injecting.
- Free from hemostasis.

Note :- Seen immediately on injection site.

Percentage of positive aspiration :- Less than 1 percent.

Alternatives :-

- Maxillary Nerve Block
- Local Infiltration.

Needle insertion :-

Needle is inserted slowly until the palatal bone is contacted in the target site.

Landmarks :-
- Second and third maxillary molars.
- Palatogingival margin of second and third maxillary molars.
- Midline of the palate.
- Towards the midline of bone approximately 1 cm from palatogingival margin.

Recommended Needle :-

25- guage short needle or 27 – guage short needle.

Orientation of bevel :-Toward the palatal soft tissue.

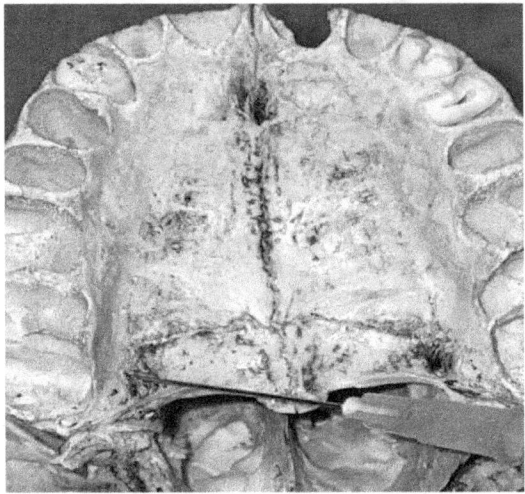

Operator position :- 7 or 8 o'clock position.

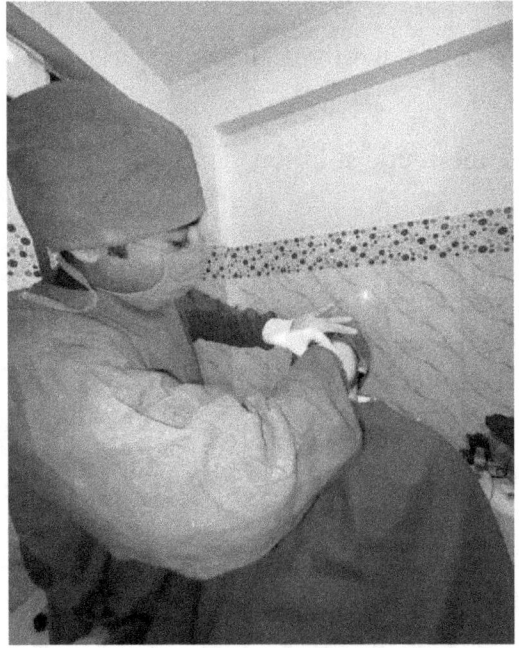

Procedure :-

Maintain the supine position of patient
↓
Locate the Greater Palatine foramen according to landmarks
↓ (Using topical antiseptic)
Clean the target area
↓
Insert the needle slowly until the palatal bone is contacted from opposite side
↓
Deposit 0.25 to 0.6 ml of solution
↓
Apply digital pressure for 30 second
↓
Look for the blanching, which appears 30 sec later
↓
Wait for 3 to 5 minute for sign & symptoms

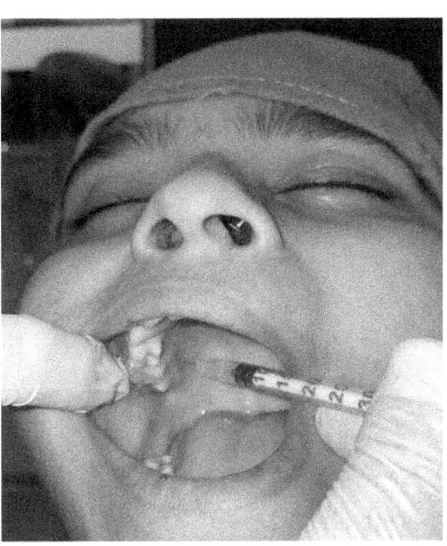

Question - What should be the ideal length of penetration in greater palatine foramen ?

Answer - 5 mm.

Sign & Symptoms :- (Subjective & Objective)
- Numbness in Posterior Palate.
- Absence of pain on instrumentation & surgical procedure is soft tissues and posterior teeth.

Safety Measures :-
- Before injecting the anesthetic solution in the target area, always aspirate.
- Make sure the needle should touch the bone while injecting.

Failure of anesthesia :-

- Injecting too far anteriorly to the foramen, may not anesthetize the target area.
- Because of overlapping fibres from nasopalatine nerve in the premolar region, there will be inadequate anesthesia on the palatal area.

Complications :-

- Ischemia and necrosis of soft tissues with the use of vasoconstrictor.
- Hematoma.
- Chances of patient discomfort if soft palate anesthetized.
- Sensation of throat closure or gagging while injecting.

MCQS - Which is specific to the atraumatic delivery of palatal injections?

   a) Pressure anesthesia

   b) Slow deposition

   c) Topical anesthesia

   d) Synringe stabilization

Answer - a

Explanation :- Syringe stabilization is especially important for palatal injections, but is fundamental to the atraumatic administration of all intra oral injections ; pressure anesthesia is unique to palatal technique. Resistance to the deposition of anesthetic solution is normal in the palatal tissue due to its highly dense nature.

MCQS - Which nerve block provides bilateral anesthesia?

   a) Grater Palatine

   b) Maxillary

   c) Anterior Middle Superior Alveolar

   d) Palatal approach –anterior superior alveolar.

Answer - d

Explanation :- The Palatal approach – anterior superior alveolar nerve block innervates the anterior branches of the anterior alveolar nerve as well as the nasopalatine nerve, producing bilateral anesthesia of the anterior hard palate and teeth from canine to canine.

MCQS - The greater palatine foramen is usually located?

   a) Mesial to the maxillary second premolar.

   b) Mesial to the maxillary first molar.

   c) Distal to the maxillary second molar.

   e) Distal to the maxillary first premolar.

Answer - c

MCQS - The deposition site the greater palatine nerve block is attained when.

   a) The needle bows slightly from the pressure.

   b) The needle comes in contact with the palatine bone.

   c) The tissue surrounding the penetration site exhibit ischemia.

   d) A small droplet of anesthetic forms against the mucous membrane.

Answer - b

Explanation :- The needle comes in gentle contact with the palatal bone when the deposition site of the greater palatine block is reached.

MCQS - What amount of local anesthetic is deposited for a greater palatine nerve block?

   a) One third of a cartridge.

   b) One half of a cartridge.

   c) Three fourth of a cartridge.

   d) 1 full cartridge.

Answer - a

MCQS - Resistance to the palatal deposition of anesthetic solution is?

   a) Intermittent

   b) Unusual

   c) Normal

   d) Rare

Answer - b

Explanation :- Resistance to the deposition of anesthetic solution is normal in the palatal tissue due to its highly dense nature.

Techniques Of Mandibular Anesthesia

Regional anesthesia of lower face and mandibular tissues by infiltration of the mandibular division of the trigeminal nerve. Mandibular nerve block involves blockage of the auriculotemporal, inferior alveolar, buccal mental incisive, mylohyoid and lingual nerves.

Inferior Alveolar Nerve Block

Note :- After local infiltration, inferior alveolar nerve block is the second most frequently used nerve block and even after administrating to the correct way, this nerve block has the highest failure rate.

This block is also known as :-

   - Classical inferior alveolar nerve block.
   - Mandibular block.
   - Inferior dental block.

Question - Why is mandibular nerve block is called inferior alveolar nerve block ?

Answer - Mandibular nerve block is called inferior alveolar nerve block because, inferior alveolar is the main branch of mandibular nerve, to anesthetize the mandibular nerve, one should block the the inferior alveolar nerve.

Nerve Anesthetized :-

- Inferior alveolar nerve.
- Incisive nerve.
- Mental nerve.
- Lingual nerve.

Note :- Pterygomandibular space has the highest chance of infection with this block.

Question - Why do mental, Incisive, and lingual nerve get anesthetized while blocking inferior alveolar nerve ?

Answer - Because mylohyoid, incisive, mental and lingual nerve is the branch of inferior alveolar nerve. The Mylohyoid nerve is derived from the inferior alveolar just before it enters the mandibular foramen.

Anesthetized area :-

- All mandibular dentition till midline.
- Ramus & body of mandible.
- Mucous membrane and buccal mucoperiosteum.
- Anterior two third of tongue & floor of oral cavity.
- Lingual soft tissues & lingual periosteum.

Indications :-

- Procedures on single or multiple teeth of the same single quadrant.
- Required to anesthetized buccal soft tissues and lingual soft tissues.
- Diagnostic and therapeutic purposes.

Contraindications :-

- Infection in injection site.
- Patients having lip and tongue biting habits.

Advantages :-

- Multiple operative procedure can done to the multiple no of teeth of the same quadrant by injecting single needle.

Disadvantages :-
- Intra orally landmarks differs patient to patient.
- By injecting this block it anesthetize a large area.
- Rate of positive aspiration is a little higher than any other intra –oral injection technique.
- Because it anesthetize the lower lip, patient may have chances for self lip biting.

Percentage of positive aspiration :- 10 to 15 %.

Anatomical Landmarks :-
- ✓ Mucobuccal fold
- ✓ Anterior border of ramus of mandible.
- ✓ External oblique ridge
- ✓ Retromolar triangle.
- ✓ Internal oblique ridge.
- ✓ Pterygomandibular ligament.
- ✓ Buccal sucking pad.
- ✓ Pterygomandibular space.

Recommended Needle :- 25 or 27 gauge long needle.

Path of insertion :- Inferior alveolar nerve.

Operator position :- 8 o'clock position.

Amount of LA solution deposited :- 1 to 1.8 ml

Technique:-

Maintain the supine position of patient
↓
While opening the mouth, the body of mandible is parallel to the floor.
↓ (apply topical anesthetic for 2 min after sterilizing the tissue)
↓
Palpate the mucobuccal fold with left index finger
↓
With the left thumb finger, make contact with the external oblique ridge posteriorly on anterior border of ramus of mandible
↓
Find the greatest depth on the anterior border of ramus of mandible, also called coronoid notch
↓
Grasp the ramus between an intra-orally placed thumb and extra orally positioned index finger
↓
Insert the needle parallel to the occlusal plane of mandibular teeth from the opposite of mouth

Enter the needle into the pterygomandibular space by bisecting the thumb
↓
Advances the needle until it makes the contact with bone on the internal surface of ramus of mandible

Withdraw the needle 1 mm & inject the solution of LA 1 to 1.8 ml for 2 minutes.
↓
Withdraw the needle, & wait for the signs & symptoms

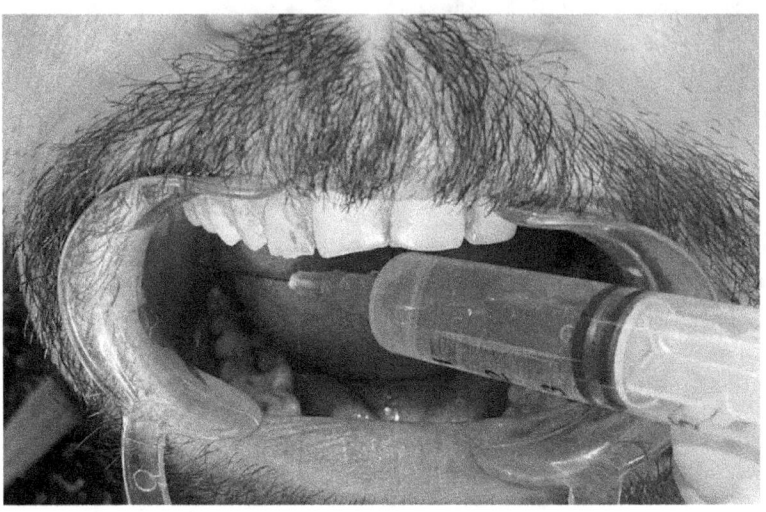

SYMPTOMS :-

Subjective :- Tingling and Numbness of lower lip.

Objective :- Absence of pain while instrumentation.

Question - What should be the average depth of penetration ?

Answer - 20 to 25 mm or $2/3^{rd}$ to $3//4^{th}$ the length of long needle.

Note :- Do not deposit the LA solution if bone is not contacted

Question - Why LA should not be deposited until it hit the bone ?

Answer - Because the penetrating needle may resting within the parotid gland near the facial nerve and a transient blockage of the facial nerve may develop if LA solution is deposited.

Complication :-

- Hematoma
- Trismus
- Transient facial paralysis

Note :- In bilateral mandibular nerve block, there is no contraindication.

A. Mandibular Nerve Block With Closed –Mouth Technique

Dr. Joseph Akinosi, in 1977 reported on a Closed –Mouth approach to mandibular block. In 1960

Dr. Sundar Varizani described the technique that was similar to Dr. Akinosi. This technique was popularized as Vazirani- Akinosi or Akinosi – Varizani because both of them contributed to this technique.

Commonly Known as :-
- Closed Mouth Technique.
- Vazirani – Akinosi Technique.
- Tuberosity technique

Nerves Anesthetized :-
- Inferior Alveolar Nerve
- Lingual Nerve
- Mental Nerve
- Incisive Nerve
- Mylohyoid Nerve
- Buccinator Nerve

Anesthetized Area :-
- All mandibular dentition till midline.
- Ramus and body of mandible.
- Mucous membrane and buccal mucoperiosteum.
- Anterior two third of tongue and floor of oral cavity.
- Lingual soft tissue and lingual periosteum.

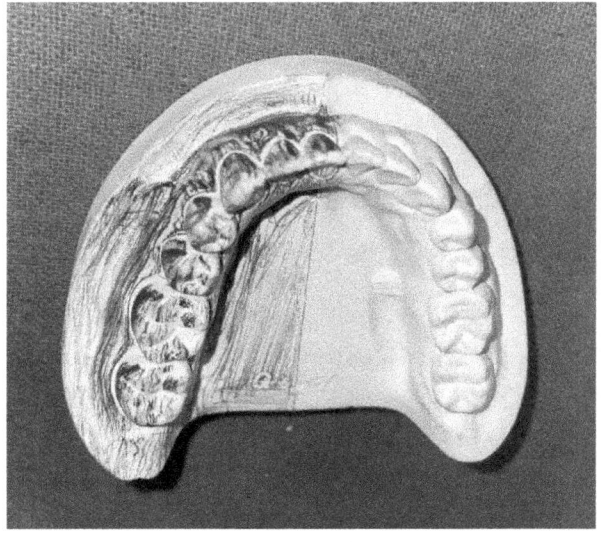

Indication :-
- ✓ Patient unable to open the mouth.
- ✓ Non- Visualization or limited visualization of inferior – alveolar nerve block landmarks.
- ✓ Teeth having multiple procedures.
- ✓ Surgical procedures on mandibular soft tisues.
- ✓ Diagnostic and therapeutic purposes.

Contraindications :-
- Infection in injection site.
- Patients having lip and tongue biting habits.
- Non- visualization to the lingual aspect of ramus.

Advantages :-
- No need to open the mouth wide.
- Atraumatic procedure.
- Less complications.
- Less aspiration rate, <10 %.
- Success of anesthetic rate is higher.
- Quick onset of anesthesia.

Disadvantages :-
- Path of insertion is difficult to visualize.
- When the needle contact the periosteum, then it is painful.
- Difficult to judge the depth of penetration.

Question - Why is it difficult to judge the depth of penetration ?

Answer - Because there are no bony contact in this technique.

Percentage of positive aspiration:- less than 10 %.

Anatomical landmarks :-
- Occluding surface of opposite posterior teeth.
- Mucogingival junction of maxillary molar teeth.
- Anterior border of ramus.

Recommended needle :- 25 or 27 gauge long needle.

Path of insertion :- In the region of inferior alveolar nerve mylohyoid nerve, lingual nerve which is medial to the ramus.

Deposition of LA :- 1.5 to 1.8 ml

Operator position :- 8 o'clock position

Technique :-

Maintain the supine position of patient
↓
Using left index finger, reflect the cheek laterally to the ramus
↓ (apply topical anesthesia for 2 minute after Sterilizing the area)
↓
Ask to occlude the teeth gently
↓
Penetrate the needle medial to ramus while the syringe is parallel to the occluding teeth
↓ (needle insertion 25 mm or 1 ½ inch)
↓
Aspirate with the syringe
↓
Deposit the anesthetic solution
↓
Wait for 5 minute to start with the procedure

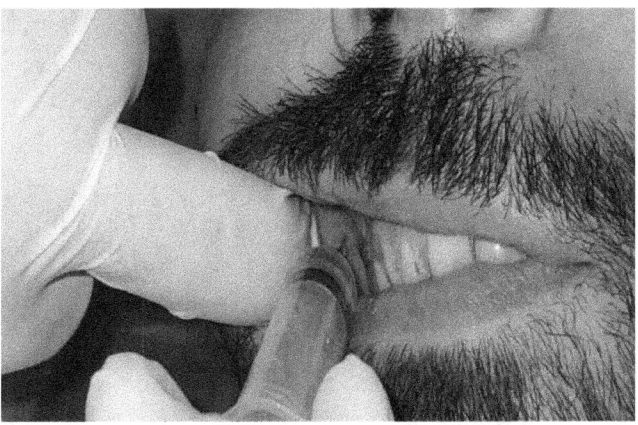

Sign & Symptoms :-

Subjective symptoms :- Tingling or numbness of lower lip, tongue.

Objective symptoms :- No response with EPT, no pain

Complications :-
- Hematoma
- Trismus
- Transient facial nerve paralysis

Question - Why Vazirani – Akinosi does not popularized ?

Answer - Because this technique realy only on soft tissue with no bony contact visualization of path and depth of insertion is difficult. Difficult in patients with pronounced Zygomatic buttress or internal oblique ridge.

Note :- Inferior alveolar nerve block is absolutely contraindicated in patients suffering from haemophilia.

B. Mandibular Nerve Block With Gow-Gates Technique

Dr. George Albert Edwards Gow Gate in 1973 came up with the new injection technique. According to hi, using this technique it anesthetizes the entire distribution of V_3 i.e., Inferior Alveolar, lingual, Buccal, Mylohyoid, Incisive, Mental, Auriculo temporal nerve.

Question - Why Gow – Gates technique popularized ?

Answer - The main advantage of Gow Gates technique is that it has high success rate. The chances of positive aspiration is very low i.e, 2% and it do not cause any problem with accessory nerves with mandibular branch.

Question - Why Gow Gate technique lost its popularization ?

Answer - High failure rate if the clinician is not well experienced. The time of onset of anesthesia is somewhat longer (5min). When compared with inferior alveolar nerve. There is a learning curve with Gow Gates technique Clinical experience is necessary to learn the technique. It has noted that the lingual and lower lip anesthesia is uncomfortable for many patients and possibly dangerous for certain individuals.

Commonly Known as :-

- Third Division Nerve Block
- Gow Gates technique
- V_3 nerve block.

Nerve Anesthetized :-

- Inferior Alveolar Nerve
- Mental Nerve
- Incisive Nerve
- Lingual Nerve
- Buccal Nerve
- Mylohyoid Nerve
- Auriculotemporal Nerve.

Anesthetized area :-

- All mandibular dentition till midline.
- Ramus and body of mandible.
- Mucous membrane and buccal mucoperiosteum.
- Anterior two third of tongue and floor of the mouth.
- Lingual soft tissue and lingual periosteum.

Indications :-

- When conventional inferior alveolar nerve block fails to anesthetize.
- When lingual soft tissue anesthesia is necessary.
- Teeth having multiple procedure.

Contraindications :-

- Infection or inflammation in infection site.
- Patients having lip and tongue biting habits.
- One who is unable to open the mouth bigger.

Advantages :-

- Less complications.
- To anesthetize the area, need single injection.
- Success of anesthetic rate is higher.
- Aspiration rate is less.

Disadvantages :-

- To anesthetize lingual and lower lip, patient feel uncomfortable.
- Operator should know the learning curve.
- Time to onset of anesthesia is longer than conventional.

Percentage of positive aspiration :- less than 2 %.

Anatomical landmarks :-

- Anterior border of ramus of mandible.
- Tendon of temporal muscle.
- Corner of mouth.
- Intertragic notch of the ear.
- External ear.

Recommended needle :- 25 to 27 gauge long needle.

Path of insertion :- just below the insertion of lateral pterygoid to the lateral side of condylar neck.

Deposition of LA :- 1.8 ml for one minute.

Operator position :- 10 o' clock position.

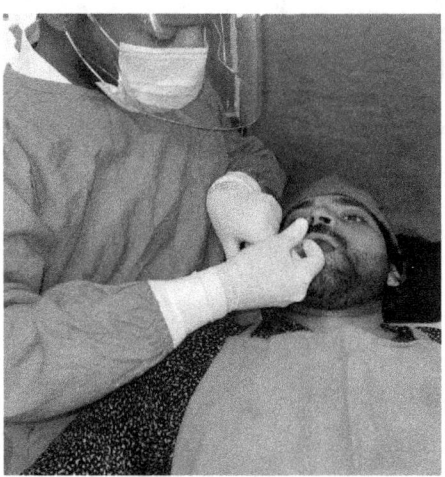

Technique :-

Maintain the supine position of the patient
↓
Place the left index finger on the coronoid notch
↓ (apply topical anesthesia for 1 minute after
Sterilizing the area)
↓
Retract the cheek on the target site
↓
From opposite side direct the syringe to the corner of mouth
↓ (after palpating tendon of temporal muscle)
From the corner of mouth, direct the syringe to the intertragic notch on injection side
↓ (draw an imaginary line from the corner of mouth
to intertragic notch)
Advance the needle until fovea region of the condylar neck is
↓ (do not exceed the depth to 25 to 27 mm)

*Withdraw the needle &reinsert if the bone contact is absent.

Aspirate the syringe and deposit the local anesthetic solution if it is negative

Ask the patient to open the mouth for 30 second

Wait for 5 to 7 minute for sign & symptoms

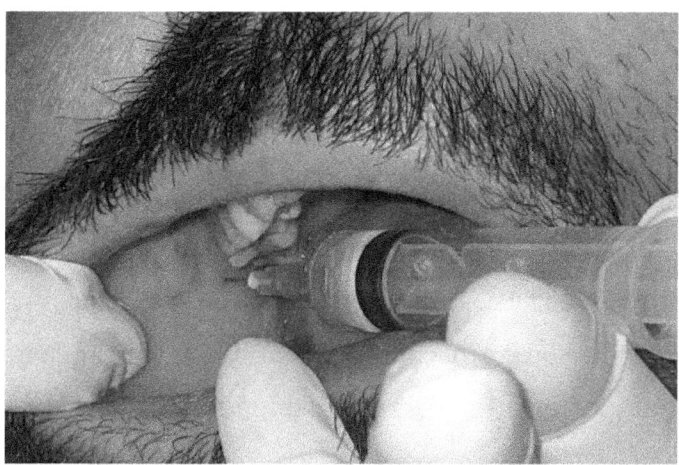

Question - Why it is instructed the patient to open the mouth for 30 second ?

Answer - Because by doing this, it allows adequate bathing of the nerve while the nerve is straightened on opening mouth. It need time because it has larger diameter (1 cm).

Subjective symptoms :- Tingling and numbness of lower lip, tongue.

Objective symptoms :- no response with EPT, no pain on instrumentation.

Complications :-
- Hematoma
- Trismus
- Temporary facial nerve paralysis
- Middle ear problem (decreased hearing, pain, inability to equilibrates ear pressure, headache).

Let's Revise :-

Question - Profound Maxillary anesthesia is more difficult to achieve than mandibularanesthesia, because the maxillary cortical plate is rather thin ?

a) Both the statement and the reason are correct but not related.

b) Both the statement and the reason are correct and related.

c) The statement is correct, but the reason is not.

d) The statement is not correct, but the reason is correct.

Answer - d

Question - The success rate of mandibular anesthesia is not attributed to which factor ?

    a) Absence of consistent landmarks.

    b) Need for multiple needle insertions.

    c) Presence of a thick mandibular cortical plate.

    d) Inability to anesthetize the core fibres of nerve.

Answer - b

Explanation :- The effect of multiple needle insertions is important to consider. When administering multiple supraperiosteal injections, a procedure that is not recommended for mandibular anesthesia.

Question - The Vazirani –Akinosi nerve block is uniquely helpful in which scenario ?

    a) The patient is unable to open her mouth more than a few mm.

    b) The patient has a history of unsuccessful inferior alveolar nerve blocks.

    c) The patient is scheduled for three procedures, all within the same quadrant.

    d) The patient's treatment plan involves the right and left mandibular incisors.

Answer - a

Explanation :- The Vazirani – Akinosi nerve block is & unique technique, because it requires a closed, not open, jaw. This technique is distinctively helpful in case where the patient is unable to open jaw.

Question - Which supplemental technique is used to rectify partial anesthesia of a lower incisor, following the administration of an otherwise successful inferior alveolar nerve block ?

    a) Intraosseous anesthesia

    b) Periodontal ligament injection

    c) Contralateral inferior alveolar nerve block

    d) Supraperiosteal injection.

Answer - d

Question - The inferior alveolar nerve block ?

    a) Is also known as the buccinators nerve block.

    b) Has the highest incidence of positive aspiration.

    c) Has a 95 % success rate in producing profound anesthesia.

    d) Is administered with the use of a 25-27 gauge short needle.

Answer - b

Question - A right – handed operator sits in which position to administer a left inferior alveolar nerve block ?

    a) 8 o'clock

    b) 9 o'clock

    c) 10 o'clock

    d) 11 o'clock

Answer - c

Explanation :- The 10 o'clock operator position is recommended for best visualization and administration of a left IANB.

Question - In most patients, the height of inferior alveolar injection lies ?

    a) 1-3 mm above the occlusal plane.

    b) 3-6 mm above the occlusal plane.

    c) 6-10 mm above the occlusal plane.

    d) 10-12 mm above the occlusal plane.

Answer - c

Question - How much of the needle is visible during the deposition of IANB ?

    a) one third

    b) one half

    c) Two third

    d) Three fourth

Answer - a

Question - Which amount of anesthetic is deposited at the inferior alveolar nerve ?

    a) 1.8 ml

    b) 1.5 ml

    c) 1.2 ml

    d) 10 ml

Answer - b

Question - Facial paralysis may develop in connection with IANB if :-

    a) The bone is contacted too forcefully.

    b) Anesthetic is deposited without bony contact.

    c) The needle comes in contact with the bone too soon.

    d) Anesthetic is deposited too far below the mandibular foramen.

Answer - b

Explanation :- Facial paralysis is possible consequence of depositing anesthetic without first making bony contact. The needle tip, in this scenario, is instead resting within the parotid gland, near the facial nerve.

Question - Which complication is extremely common, after the dissipation of IANB ?

a) Hematoma

b) Mild trismus

c) Blepharoptosis

d) Facial paralysis.

Answer - b

Question - Bone is gently contacted in each injection, Except one. Which is Exception ?

a) Buccal nerve block

b) Vazirani – Akinosi Mandibular nerve block.

c) Inferior alveolar nerve block

d) Gow – Gates Mandibular nerve block.

Answer - b

Question - Which disadvantage is attributed to the Gow- Gates Mandibular nerve block ?

a) Low success rate.

b) High incidence of positive aspiration.

c) Hesitancy on the part of the operator to learn the technique.

d) Partial anesthesia related to unanesthetized accessory innervation.

Answer - c

Question - The onset of anesthesia, following a Gow- Gates Mandibular block, is anticipated within ?

a) 2min

b) 3 min

c) 4 min

d) 5 min

Answer - d

Explanation :- The onset of anesthesia, following a Gow –Gates mandibular block, oocurs within 5 minutes. This slightly delayed onset is primarily attributed to the nerve trunk size and the distance of the nerve trunk from the deposition site.

Question - Which needle is recommended for a vazirani – Akinosi mandibular block ?

    a) 25 gauge short

    b) 27gaugeshort

    c) 25 gauge short

    d) 27 gauge long.

Answer - c

Question - Which intra oral landmark guides the Gow Gates Mandibular block ?

    a) Coronoid notch

    b) Mucogingival junction of maxillary second or third molar.

    c) Mesiolingual cusp of maxillary second molar.

    d) Most posterior mandibular molar.

Answer - c

Question - After administering the Gow – Gates mandibular nerve block ?

    a) Ask the patient keep his / her mouth open for 1-2 min.

    b) Lower the patient from the supine to the tendelenburg position.

    c) Wait at least 10 min before commencing the dental procedure.

    d) Maintain gentle finger pressure directly over the injection site for 2 min.

Answer - a

Question - In the Vazirani- Akinosi technique, the bevel of the needle is positioned away from the**:-**

    a) Midline, toward bone.

    b) bone, toward the midline.

    c) Floor of the mouth, toward palate.

    d) Palate, toward floor of mouth.

Answer - b

Question - Objective signs of inferior alveolar nerve block are seen in :-

    a) Unilateral midline between premolars and incisors.

    b) Bilaterally between premolars and incisors.

    c) Unilateral midline between second molar and incisor.

    d) Bilateral midline between second molar and incisor.

Answer - a

Question - Which of the following technique of local anesthesia requires extra oral landmarks ?

    a) High tuberosity approach

    b) Fischer 123

    c) Gow Gates

    d) Vazirani Akinosi

Answer - c

Question - Which is the Extra-oral landmark for Gow Gates technique of mandibular nerveblock ?

    a) Corner of mouth.

    b) Intertragic notch.

    c) Both of the above.

    d) None of the above.

Answer - c

Question - In the extra – oral technique for mandibular nerve block, the needle after contacting the pterygoid plate is directed ?

    a) Anteriorly

    b) Posteriorly

    c) Superiorly

    d) Inferiorly

Answer - b

Question - In case of Gow Gates technique, the target area is :-

    a) Neck of condyle.

    b) Head of the condyle.

    c) Medial side of the ramus.

    d) Lateral side of the condyle.

Answer - a

Question - Improper direction of the needle insertion during inferior alveolar nerve block results in :-

    a) Facial nerve paralysis.

    b) Paraesthesia.

    c) Hematoma.

    d) Trismus.

Answer - a

Question - A patient presents with trismus. which of the following technique will block mylohyoid nerve, incisive and long buccal nerve ?

    a) Akinosi's technique.

    b) Gow Gate's technique

    c) Vblock technique

    d) Conventional inferior alveolar nerve block.

Answer - a

Lingual Nerve Block

No other common

Nerve anesthetized :- Lingual nerve.

Anesthetized area :-

- Soft tissue include mucosa and mucoperiosteum on the lingual side of the mandible.
- Floor of the mouth including two – third of the tongue.
- All mandibular dentition till midline.
- Ramus and body of mandible.

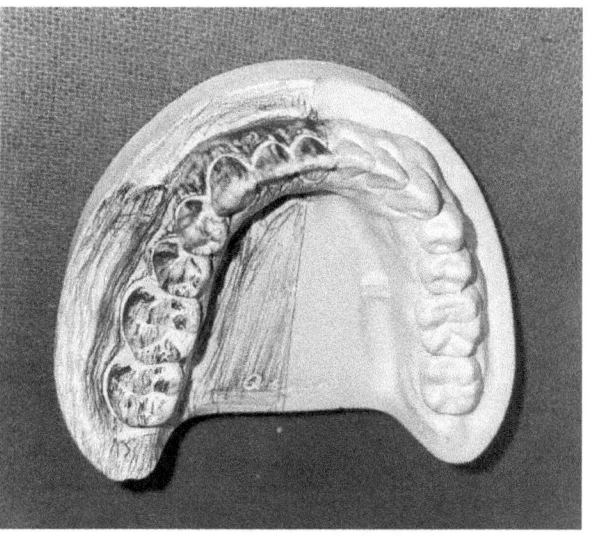

Indications :-

- Procedure on single or multiple teeth of the same single quadrant.
- Required to anesthetized buccal soft tissues and lingual soft tissues.
- Procedures requires on the anterior two third of the tongue, floor of the oral cavity.
- Mucous membrane on the lingual side of the mandible.
- Diagnostic and therapeutic purposes.

Contraindications :-

Infection in injection site or inflammation.

Advantages :-

Disadvantages :-

Because it anesthetize the anterior two third of the tongue, patient may bite his /her tongue unintentionaly.

Percentage of positive aspiration :- 10 – 15 %

Anatomical landmarks :-

- Mucobuccal fold.
- Anterior border of ramus of mandible.
- External oblique ridge.
- Retromolar triangle.
- Internal oblique ridge.
- Pterygomandibular ligament.
- Buccal sucking pad.
- Pterygomandibular space.

Recommended needle :- 25 to 27 gauge long needle.

Path of insertion :- Lingual nerve.

Operator position :- 8'o clock position.

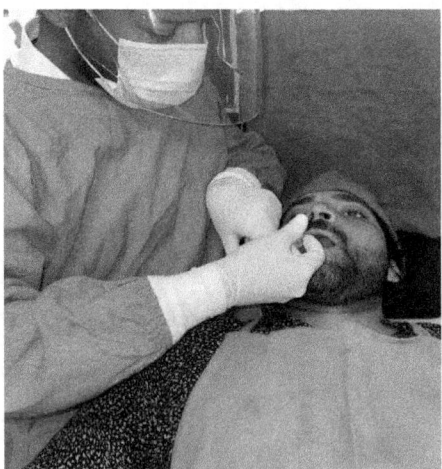

Amount of LA deposition :- 0.5 ml.

Technique :-

Maintain the supine position of the patient
↓
While opening the mouth, the body of mandible is parallel to the floor
↓ (apply topical anesthetic for 2 min after sterilizing the tissue)
Palpate the mucobuccal fold with left index finger.
↓
With the left thumb finger, make contact with external oblique ridge posteriorly or anterior border of ramus of mandible
↓
Find the greatest depth on the anterior border of ramus of mandible, also called coronoid notch
↓
Grasp the ramus of mandible between an intra-orally placed thumb finger and extra-orally positioned index finger
↓
Insert the needle parallel to the occlusal plane of mandible teeth from the opposite side of mouth.
↓ (Pull the needle 1 mm out & insert around 10 mm)
Advances the needle until it makes the contact with bone on the internal surface of ramus of mandible
↓
Deposit the solution 0.5 ml
↓
Withdraw the needle out and wait for the sign & symptoms

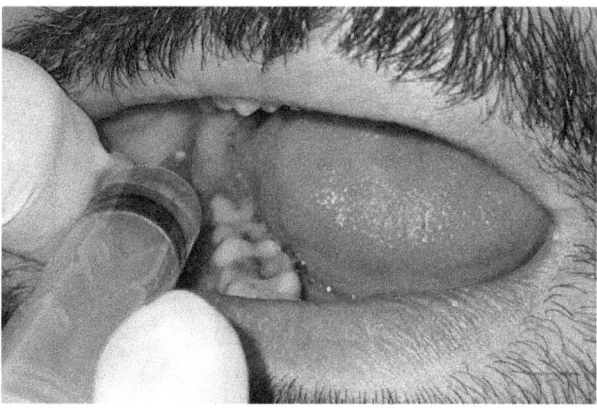

*(Same technique as IANB with just a small change)

Subjective Symptoms :- Tingling & numbness of anterior two third of tongue & poor of the mouth.

Objective Symptoms :- Absence of pain on instrumentation.

Question - Noticing of numbness in the lateral part of lower lip, chin and the tongue. This is due to the infiltration of the :-

   a) Posterior Superior Alveolar Nerve.
   b) Lingual Nerve.
   c) Nerve to mylohyoid.
   d) Buccal Nerve.

Answer - b

Explanation :- The lingual nerve passes forward into the submandibular region from the infratemporal fossa by running beneath the origin of the superior constrictor muscle, which is attached to the posterior border of the mylohyoid line on the mandible. Here, it is closely related to the last molar tooth & is liable to be damaged in cases of clumsy extraction of an impacted third molar.

Buccal Nerve Block

Also known as :

   - Long buccal nerve block.
   - Buccinator

Nerve Anesthetized area :- Buccal Nerve.

Anesthetized area :-

   - Mucous membrane and mucoperiosteum of mandibular molar on the buccal surface area.

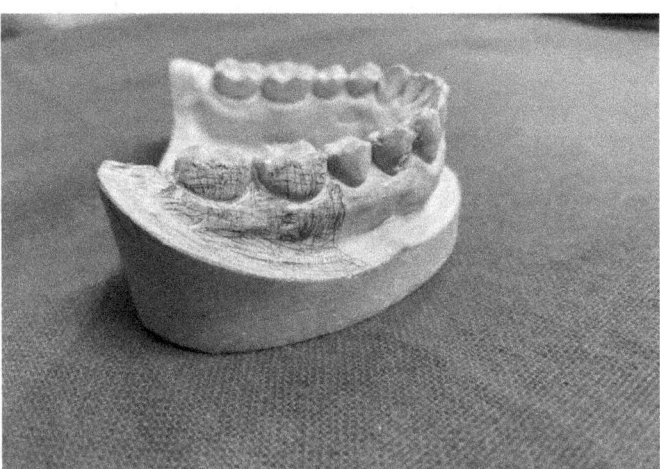

Indications :-

   - When dealing with buccal mucosa and to enhance the effect of inferior alveolar nerve block.

Contraindications :-

   - Inflammation and infection in injection site.

Advantages :-
- Easy to administer
- It has good success rate.

Disadvantages :-
- Patient will complain of pain if the needle is in contact with the periosteum.

Percentage of positive aspiration :- 0.7 %

Amount of solution deposit :- 0.25 ml to 0.5 ml of LA.

Target area :- Buccal nerve.

Needle insertion :- Distal to the third molar.

Landmarks :-
- External oblique ridge
- Retromolar triangle

Recommended needle :- 25 or 27 gauge long needle.

Orientation of bevel :- Towards bone.

Operator position :- 8 o'clock position.

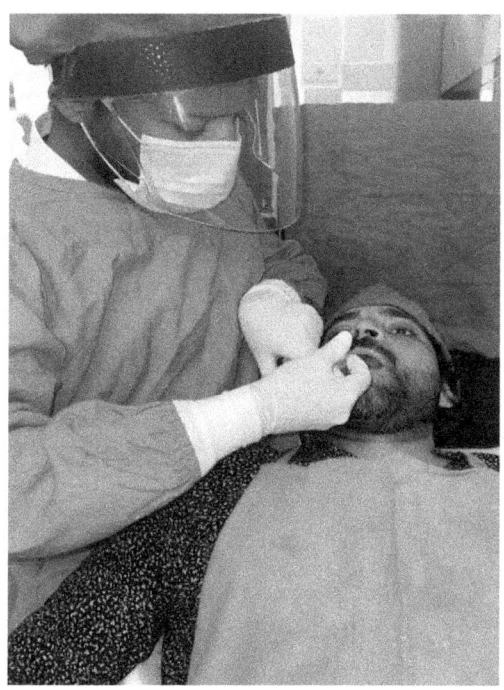

Procedure :-

Maintain supine position of the patient
↓ (apply antiseptic & topical anesthetic for 1 to 2 Minutes).

Pull the buccal soft tissues of target site.
↓
Direct the syringe aligning to the occlusal plane bucally
↓
Insert the syringe distal to the third molar or insert the syringe directly to the retromolar triangle.
↓
Wait for 5 minute to achieve the sign & symptoms.

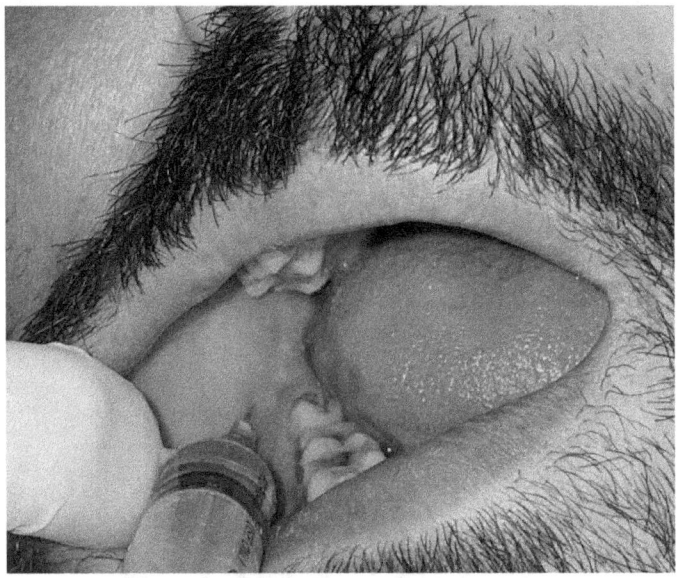

Subjective symptoms :- No subjective symptoms.

Objective symptoms :- No pain while instrumentation.

Question - The bevel of the needle in the buccal nerve block is positioned toward the :-

a) Bone
b) Cheek
c) Tongue
d) Occlusion.

Answer - a

* Towards anterior border of ramus.

Question - Anesthesia of the buccal nerve is contraindicated for which procedure ?

   a) Placing a matrix band around the mandibular third molar.

   b) Restoring a carious cavitation in the second mandibular molar.

   c) Placing a rubber dam clamp around second mandibular molar.

   d) Scaling subgingival calculus deposits from the first mandibular molar.

Answer - b

* The buccal nerve block is contraindicated for restorative procedure, which do not requke the manipulation of the buccal soft tissues adjacent to the mandibular molar.

Question - The penetration site of the buccal nerve block is:-

   a) Distal & buccal to the last molar.

   b) Distal & lingual to the last molar.

   c) Mesial and buccal to the last molar.

   d) Mesial and lingual to the last molar.

Answer - a

Mental Nerve Block

Note :- No other common name for mental nerve block.

Nerve anesthetized :- Mental nerve.

Anesthetized area :-

   - Lower lip till midline
   - Buccal mucous membrane
   - Chin

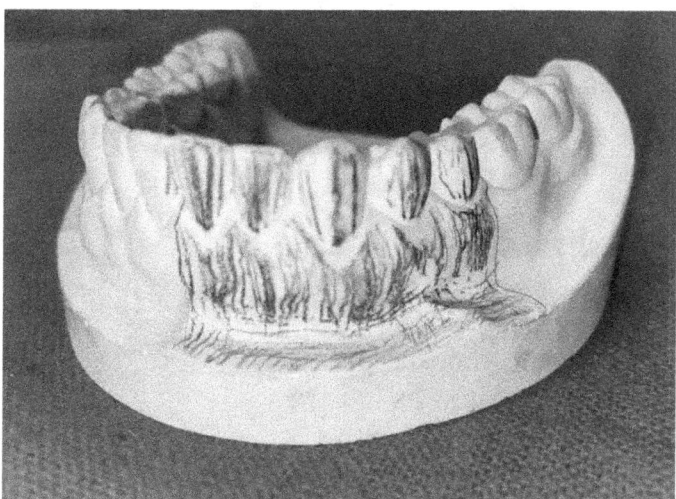

Indications :-

   - Where the inferior alveolar nerve is not needed.

- Lower lip surgery or procedure to be done in soft tissue anterior to the mental foramen.

Contraindications :-

- Inflammations or infection in the injection site.

Advantages :-

- Easy to administer.
- Tissue do not traumatized.
- It also has high success rate.
- One can work on a small soft tissue area without inferior alveolar nerve block.

Disadvantage :-

- High chances of hematoma formation.

Percentage of positive aspiration :- 5.7 %

Amount of solution deposited :- 0.5 to 1 ml of LA.

Target area :- Mental nerve

Needle insertion :- Into the mucobuccal fold anterior to mental foramen.

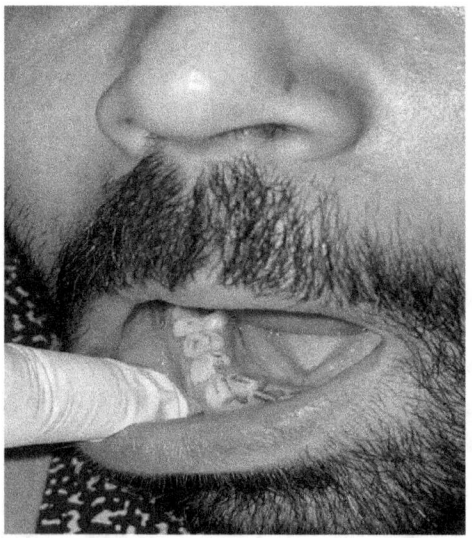

Anatomical landmarks :-

- Bicuspid teeth in mandibular arch

*Position of mental foramen is at the apex and anterior to second premolar root.

Recommended needle :- 25 or 27 gauge short needle.

Bevel orientation :- Towards bone.

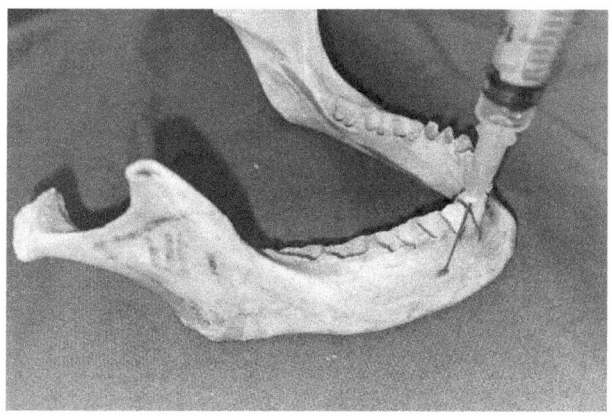

Operator position :- 7 o'clock position.

Procedure :-

Maintain the supine position of the patient
↓ (apply antiseptic and topical anesthetic for 1 minute)
Pull the buccal soft tissue and lower lip outward
↓
Locate the apex of second premolar tooth of the prepared side.
↓
Insert the needle around 1 inch into mucolabial fold until the tip of needle reaches anterior to the apex of second premolar
↓
Deposit the solution of LA.
↓
Wait for 3 minutes for sign & symptoms

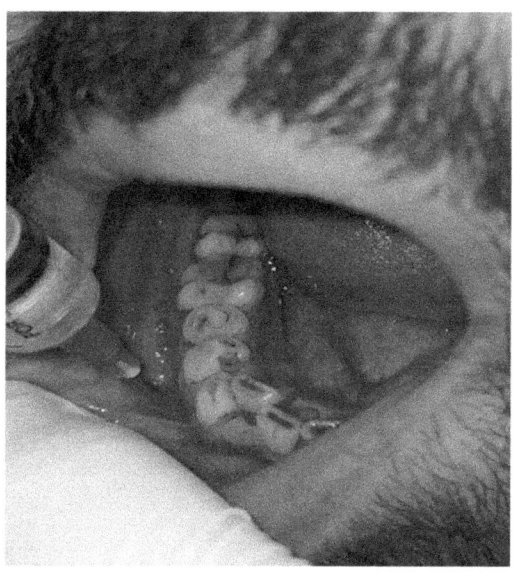

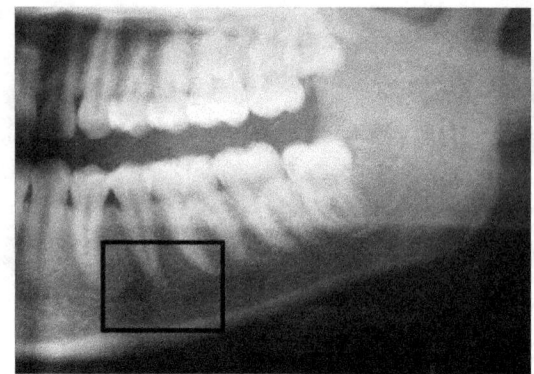

Subjective symptoms :- Tingling & numbness in the soft tissue of chin & lower lip.

Objective symptoms :- Painless during instrumentation.

Complications :-

- Hematoma.
- Paresthesia of lip and chin.

Question - Picture based question.

Question - In anesthetizing lower anterior all of the following are indicated except :-

a) Fischer 123 technique.

b) Classical inferior alveolar nerve block.

c) Mental nerve block

d) Incisive nerve block

Answer - c

Incisive Nerve Block

Also known as inappropriately mental nerve block although incisive and mental nerve block is two different injection technique.

Nerve anesthetized :- Mental and Incisive nerve.

Anesthetized area :-

- Lower lip till midline of the target area.
- Buccal mucous membrane.
- Chin.
- Central incisor, lateral incisor, canine & premolar teeth on the target side.
- Overlying structures anterior to the mental foramen.

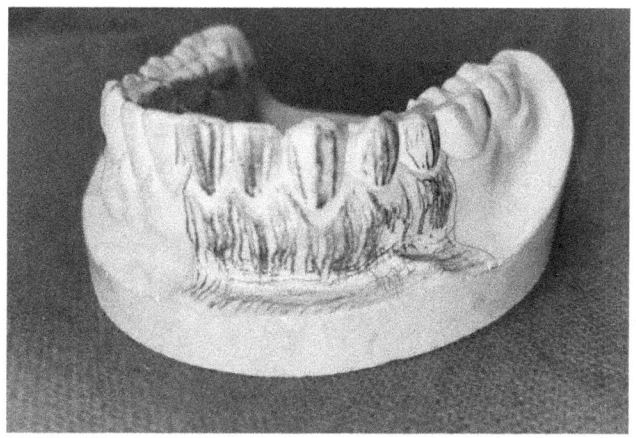

Indications :-

- When the inferior alveolar nerve is not needed.
- Lower lip surgery or procedure to be done in soft tissue anterior to the mental foramen.
- The structures present on the labial surface of mandible.
- Dental procedures in respective of central incisor, lateral incisor, canine and premolar.

Contraindications :-

- Inflammation or infection in the injection site.

Advantages :-

- Success rate is quite good.
- Operator can avoid bilateral inferior alveolar nerve block.
- Without administrating lingual nerve block, it provides pulpal and osseous anesthesia.

Disadvantages :-

- Sometimes complete anesthesia may not provide with this injection technique.
- It does not provide the lingual anesthesia.

Question - Why partial anesthesia may develop at midline ?

Answer - Partial anesthesia may develop at the midline because the nerve fibers present on both the side of middle may overlap each other.

Question - What can operator do for complete pulpal anesthesia in such situation ?

Answer - Operator can locally infiltrate the anesthetic solution of 0.9 ml in buccal surface of lower central incisor.

Percentage of positive aspiration :- 5.7 %

Needle insertion :- Mucobuccal fold at or just anterior to mental foramen.

Landmarks :- Mandibular bicuspid teeth and mucobuccal fold.

Recommended needle :- 27 gauge short needle is recommended.

Orientation of bevel :- Toward bone.

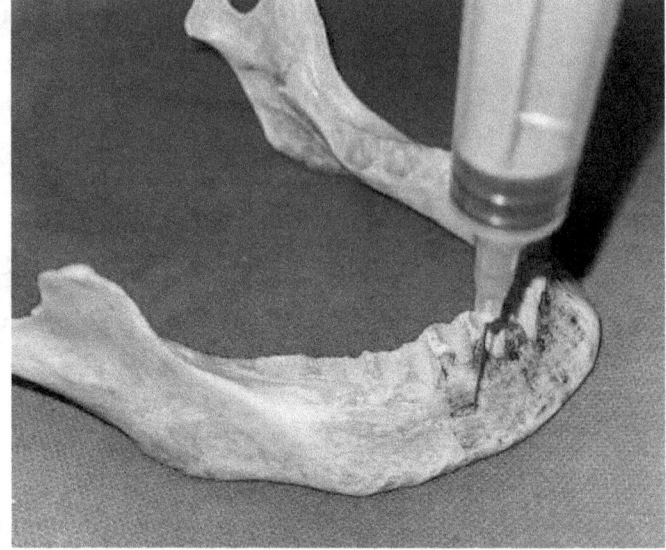

Operator position :- 7 o'clock position.

Solution deposit :- 0.6 ml.

Procedure :-

Maintain the semi supine position of the patient
↓
Apply antiseptic and topical anesthic for 1 minute
↓
Pull the Buccal soft tissue and lower lip outward
↓
Locate the apex of second premolar tooth of the prepared side
↓
Insert the needle around 5-6 mm into mucobuccal fold except the needle point should penetrate into mental foramen the mental nerve will automatically be anesthetized at the same time
↓
Deposit the solution of local anesthesia
↓
Wait for 3 minute for sign and symptoms

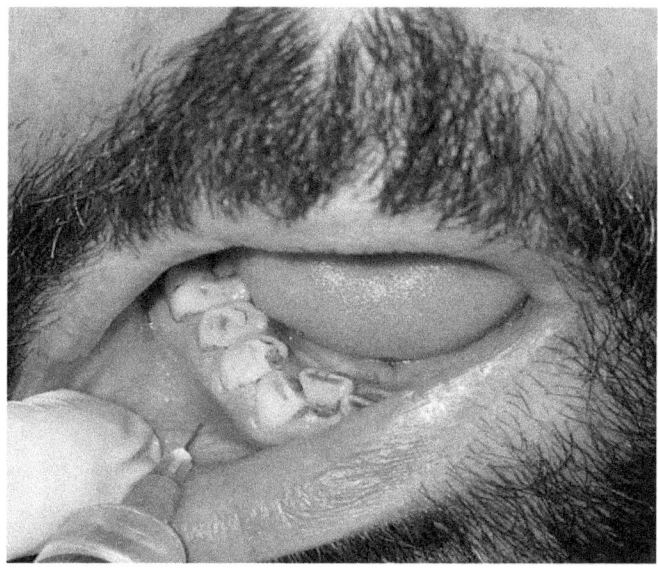

Subjective Symptoms :- tingling and numbness in the soft tissue of thin and lower lip or may not

Objective Symptoms :- Painless during instrumentation

Complications :-

- Hematoma
- Paresthesia of lip or chin

Question - How does hematoma forms and how will you treat ?

Answer - Hematoma forms when the blood exit the needle puncture site into the buccal fold. Eventually it converts to bluish discoloration and tissue swelling at injection site. To treat this, apply digital pressure for 2 minutes at the site.

Question -The Inclusive nerve block does not anesthetize which tooth ?

- Molar
- Incisor
- Canine
- Premolar

Answer - a

Explanation :- Because the fibre of Incisive nerve does not supply to the molar region and the molar tooth.

Question - Which facilitates a successful incisive nerve block ?

   a) The needle must gently penetrate the mental foramen

   b) The bevel of the needle must be positioned away from the bone

   c) The operator must deposit one fourth of the anesthetic cartridge

   d) The operator must apply gentle finger pressure over the injection site

Answer - d

Question - Nerves anesthetised in incisive nerve block are:

   a) Incisive and mental nerve

   b) Incisive nerve only

   c) Mental and Inferior alveolar

   d) Incisive and Inferior alveolar nerve

Answer - a

Question - A man of 40 year comes in a dental clinic with the complain of pain in lower jaw. The dentist diagnoses at carious last molar and decided to extract under local anesthesia. After administrating LA, he extracted the tooth. After this patient come with the complain of numbness in the lateral part of lower lip, chin & tongue. This is due to infiltration of :-

   a) Buccal nerve

   b) Nerve to mylohyoid

   c) Lingnal nerve

   d) Posterior superior alveolar nerve

Answer - c

Explanation :- Injury to the lingual nerve :- the lingual nerve passes forward into the submandibular region from the infratemporal fossa by running beneath the origin of the superior constrictor muscle, which is attached to the posterior border of mylohyoid line on the mandible there, it is closely related to the last molar tooth and is liable to the damaged in cases of clumsy extraction of an impacted third molar.

Exodontia

Introduction:-

The ideal tooth extraction is: The painless removal of the whole tooth or tooth roots, with minimal trauma to the investing tissues, so that the bone heals uneventfully and no post – operative prosthetic problem is created – Geoffrey L Howe.

OR

Exodontia can be defined as painless removal of a tooth or tooth root from its socket with minimal injury to the bone and surrounding structure so that post-operative waling is uneventful – Abhay N Datarkar.

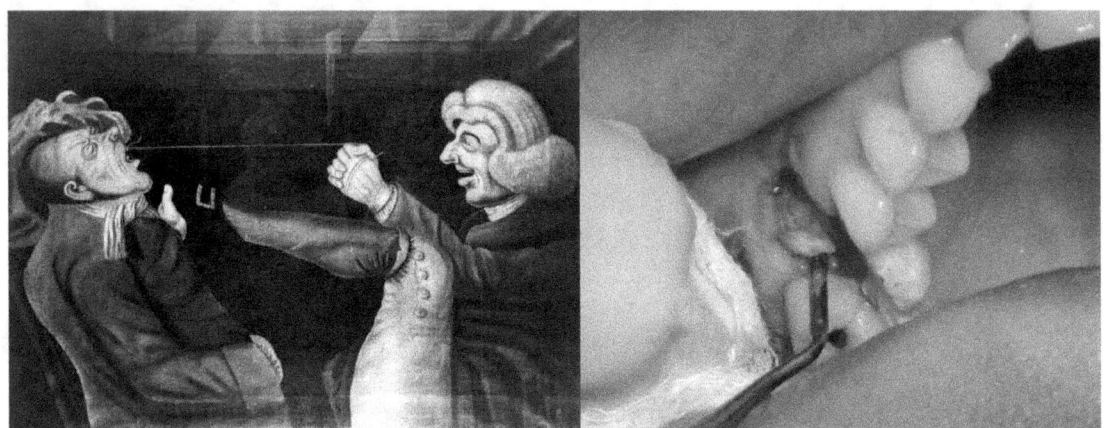

Fig 1. Traditional method vs Modern method

Factors Complicating Dental Extraction:

1. Restriction by both cheeks, upper and lower lips such as fibrosis.
2. Movement of lower jaw
3. Movement of Tounge
4. Structure like floor of mouth, tongue soft palate & hard palate and even the tonsil may be damaged.
5. Communicaton of mouth with pharynx & larynx
6. Flodding of oral laving with micro organisms

Indications:

- Dental caries in 48.8% (Allen 1999), abscess
- Periodontal diseases, in 40.7% cases to prevent alveolar ridge resorption
- If tooth is having pulp pathology or endodontic therapy is not possible
- Teeth or tooth having apical pathology and it fails to respond to all conservative measures
- Orthodontic reasons, few teeth may require extraction

- Over retained deciduous tooth
- Prosthetic purpose
- Impacted teeth
- Supernumerary teeth
- Tooth in line of fracture
- Teeth in relation to bony pathology
- Root fragments
- Teeth prior to irradiation
- Focal sepsis
- Esthetics
- Economic considerations
- Unrestorable tooth
- Teeth directly involved by cyst and tumor
- Fracture of large restoration
- Dental erosion, attrition or abrasion.
- Abnormalities of tooth development, example- hypoplasia, germination.
- Root resorption
- Dislocation of tooth from the socket due to trauma.
- Crown or root fracture

Contraindications

- May be relative or absolute contraindication relative contraindication is in other words patient can undergo extraction once the under lying condition is treated or controlled e.g. Diabetes or disease.

Absolute contraindications under no condition extraction can be done of

Relative Contraindication

Local factors

- Presence of oral infection such as vincent's angina, herpetic gingivostomatitis.
- Localised periapical pathology
- Acute pericoronitis
- Malignant disease
- Irradiated jaw
- Acute cellulitis
- ANUG

Systemic factors
- Acute blood dyscrasias as Hemophilia Anemia
- Agranulocytosis
- Non treated coagulopathies as congenital or acquired
- Adrenal insufficiencies
- Within 6 months of Mayocardial Infarction
- Pregnancy (avoid in 1st and 3rd trimester)
- Patients on steroid therapy
- Diabetes
- Hypertension
- Medically compromised patient as T.B
- Addison's disease
- Fever of unexplained origin such as sub-acute bacterial endocarditis
- Nephritis
- During menstruation cycle, as there is more bleeding patient is mentally and nervously not so stable.
- Psychosis

Absolute Contraindication

Local Factor
- Teeth involved in anterio-venous malformations example. Central haemangioma

Systemic Factor
- Leukemia
- Renal failure
- Cirrhosis of liver
- Cardiac failure

Pre-Operative Assessment

The old saying in carpentry, which is also apt fan oral surgery

Measure twice, cut once

This assessment is divided into four parts

1. Level of anxiety: Anxiety may be because of fear from pain the surgical procedure is to be done.

2. Health status of patient: Assessment to rule out any contraindication and precautions to be taken pre and post operatively

3. Clinical assessment: Status of mouth appearing

4. Contraindication of Crown: Present absent, fractured carious that may effect the forceps applications restored may weaken the tooth and make it susceptible to fracture

- Westing diseases
- Accessibility of tooth
- Status of root: Size, shape, number, structure
- Fractured, ankylosis, mobility, resorption, hypercementosis or other pathology
- Surrounding structures condition of adjacent teeth, periapical disease and other pathology deposits around tooth so as to prevent damage to adjacent structures.
- Radiographic assessment: Evaluation of crown, root and surrounding shape and

Principles Of Extraction

Forceps are used for the following purposes:

Mechanical principles of extraction:

1) Expansion of bony socket:

    Five types of motions are used to expand the bony socket.

    i) Apical pressure to displace the centre of teeth

    ii) Buccal force to expand buccal crestal bone

    iii) Lingnal force to expand lingnal crestal bone

    iv) Rotational force to cause intra bony expansion

Note: This force is applicable only for tooth having single conical root.

v) Fractional force at the end to remove the teeth from the socket after achieving adequate bony expansion for removal of tooth from the socket, on can consider the tooth itself like a dilating instrument. The tooth should be grasped with the help of appropriate force. The shape of root should be such that, one can easily dilate expand the socket for the complete removal from its socket.

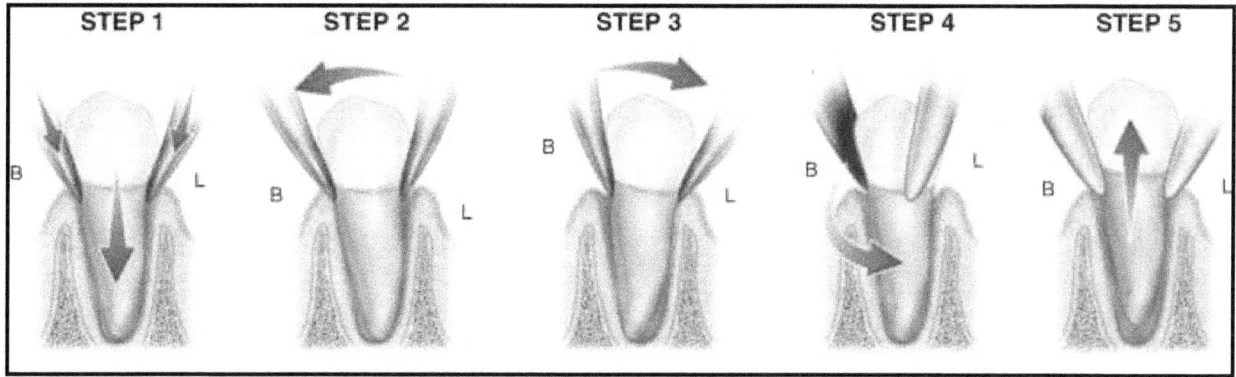

Apical Pressure Buccal / Labial Force Palatal /Lingual Force Rotational Force Tractional Force

Fig 2. Expansion of bony socket

Note: The expansion depends on the elasticity of bone.

- Maximum expansion is seen in younger age group

- Minimum expansion is seen with older age group

- During expansion multiple small fractures of buccal or lingual or inter-radicular separated can occur as age in elasticity or bone decreases.

Question - How can one minimize or reduce bony fragments ?

Answer - These bony fragments usually retain the periosteal attachment and should be minimized by digital compression at the completion of the extraction.

Question - Is there any indication for removal of loose bony fragments ?

Answer - The bony fragments which have lost more than half of these periosteal attachment should be removed from the extraction site.

Question - Why is it indicated to remove the loose bony fragments which has lost its half of periosteal attachment ?

Answer - Because their blood supply will be hampered that they will not be able to maintain its blood supply and will necrose this devitalized bony fragments cause post extraction hemorrhage, delayed healing and chances of would infection along with pain.

2) Use of lever and fulcrum: For removal of teeth out of its socket along the path of least resistance. This is done using elevators.

3) Insertion of wedge: Between the bony surface and outer surface of root, thus causing the tooth to rise in its socket. (i.e between root surface and cortical bone)

Preoperative Assessment

    1. Take history of the following

   - General disease

   - Anxiety

   - Resistance of inhalational anesthesia

   - Previous experience with extraction

    2. Status of oral hygiene

   - Use of mouth rinse

   - Oral prophylaxis

    3. Examining the tooth clinically

    4. Examining and cavity after prosthesis on any other condition

Importance For Preoperative Radiographs:

- To plan whether to remove the tooth by sectioning
- To know the difficulty index
- To know the periodontal problem, sclerosis, hypercementosis
- Close approximation with important anatomical structures
- To know the anatomy of root
- Relation of 3rd molar
- Misplaced crown
- Abnormal crown
- Delayed eruption
- Trauma to tooth, tooth fracture, root fracture, alveolar bone
- Isolated and unopposed maxillary molars
- Dental or dentoalveolar deformities: like- osteitis deformans, hypercementosis, cleido- cranial dysostosis, hooked root, therapeutic irradiation, osteopetrosis
- Pathology

Radiographic Requirements Of Pre Extraction:

- To know abnormal no of roots
- To know abnormal shape of roots
- Germination or fusion
- Wherether the tooth is ankylosed or not
- Extending caries into roots or root mass not
- Whether root is fractured or not
- Whether root is resorbed
- Hypercementosis of root
- Unfavourable root pattern
- Impacted teeth
- Pathological lesions
- Bony sclerosis

Careful interpretation of the radiograph may also reveal the possibility of the following complcations

- Involvement or close approximation of any of the nerve like – mental, inferior alveolar
- Pathological lesions
- Forming oro-antral communication
- Slippage of tooth/root into maxillary antrum

- Maxillary tuberosity fracture

Extraction procedure can be of two type

   i) Intraalveolar exodontia/closed method of extraction

   ii) Transalveolar exodontia /open method of extraction

Extraction is a surgical procedure or surgical operation that involves the bony and soft tissues of the oral cavity restricted by lips, cheeks, tongue, saliva, blood and movements of mandible, communication of mouth with the pharynx and larynx. Flooding of the oral cavity with micro-organisms.

Patient

   a) Stand erect

   b) Distribute the weight on both feet

   c) Force should not be applied with hand it is delivered with arm

   d) Application of force without stress to shoulder and back

   e) Operating box

Sometimes the operator must stands behind the patient sometimes the operator must stand upon operating box to achieve appropriate height.

Question- What should be the height of dental chair while extraction ?

Answer– For maxillary arch – 8 cm or 3 inch below the shoulder level & for mandibular arch – 16 cm or 6 inch below the shoulder level of operator.

Question- What should be the angulation of chair while extraction ?

Answer- For maxillary teeth 45-60 degree for mandibular teeth – parallel to 10 degree

Role of opposite hand:

- Helps to reflect the soft tissue
- Helps to compress socket
- Protects the other teeth
- Helps in stabilizing patient head
- Supports alveolar bone
- Tactile information

Role of assistant

- Helps the operator to gain access and visualize the field
- Helps in suctioning
- Helps to support the mandible
- Support the head
- Protect the teeth of opposite arch

- Help to pass the instrument

Principles of elevators

    a) Lever principle

    b) Wedge principle

    c) Wheel and axle principle

Lever Principle

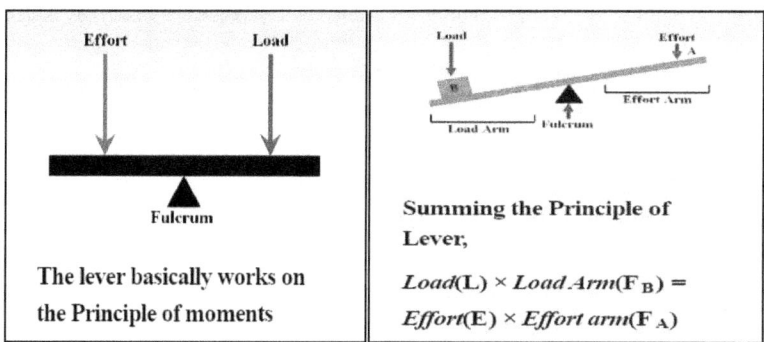

Fig. 3

There are three components; fulcrum, power and weight

- fulcrum lies between the effort arm and load arm while extracting any tooth/teeth.

- power represents handle.

- Weight is represented by beaks of elevator. In this mechanism modest force is transmitted at long arm so that the mechanical advantage is delivered at the short arm.

(Long arm is power and short arm is weight)

Hence, we get the law of levers as,

$$\frac{L}{E} = \frac{F_A}{F_B}, \text{ where}$$

→ F_A: Effort on Fulcrum

→ F_B: Load on Fulcrum

→ L: Load and E: Effort

Rearranging,

$$\Rightarrow \frac{L}{E} = \frac{F_A}{F_B}$$

Fig.4

$\dfrac{L}{E}$ is called Mechanical Advantage which can be computed from ratio of the distances from the fulcrum to where the input force (E) and output force (L) are applied to the lever

Whereas, Velocity ratio (V.R.) is the ratio of the length of the load arm to the length of the effort arm

Fig.5

Most commonly used principle

Note: In order to get mechanical advantage, effort arm must be longer than resistance arm

Used to remove roots

Example – Straight elevator

- Cryer's elevator
- Apexo elevator

Small force, large movement

Large force, small movement

Resistance arm = short arm

Effort arm = long arm

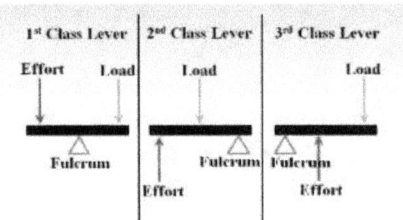

The figure shows the classification of the three categories of lever

Types of lever:

1st class lever: Fulcrum is located between input effort and output load.

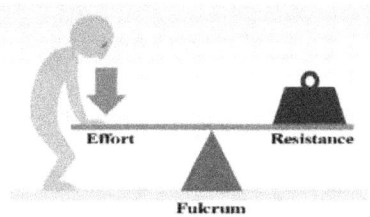

In this kind of levers, the Fulcrum is in between the effort and the load or resistance

Seesaw is a very common example of Class 1 lever

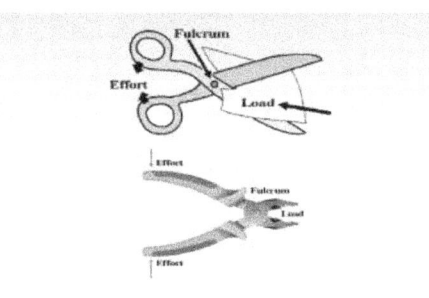

Other examples of class 1 lever pair of scissors, pliers etc

For class 1 levers, the Mechanical Advantage(M.A) and Velocity Ratio(V.R) can have any value: either greater than, equal to or less than 1

2nd class lever: Fulcrum is located on other end opposite to input and output load is located between these two forces.

In this type of levers, the fulcrum and effort at the two ends and load or resistance is somewhere in between

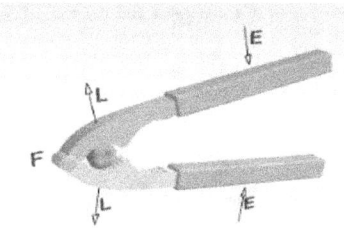

A nutcracker is a common example of Class 2 lever

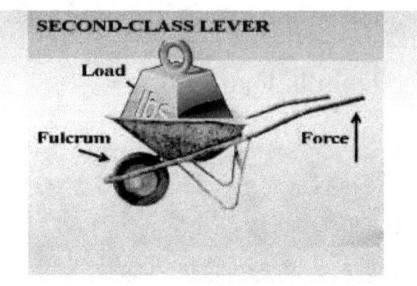

A wheelbarrow, used to carry load, is another example of Class 2 lever

For a Class 2 lever, the Mechanical Advantage (M.A) and Velocity Ratio (V.R) values are always greater than one

3rd class lever: Input effort is greater than output load

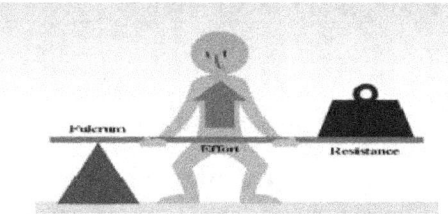

In this type, the fulcrum and the load are at the two ends of the lever and the effort is somewhere in between

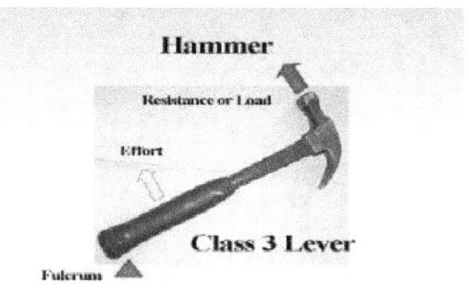

Hammer is a very common example of Class 3 levers

Other examples of class 3 levers are broom, fishing rod etc

For Class 3 levers, the Mechanical Advantage (M.A.) and the Velocity Ratio (V.R.) are always less than one

Mechanical advantage:

Resistance arm: effort arm

Resistance arm x short arm = effort arm x long arm

Long arm = 3/4 of total arm

Short arm = ¼ of total arm

R x 1/4th = E x ¾ th

R/E = ¼ x 4/3 = 3/1

R = 3E

R/E = 3/1

Mechanical advantage = 3

Wedge Principle:

Wedge is used to split or expand or to displace. It is a movable inclined plane, at the right angles a large resistance is applied to the effort, at the base, the effort is applied and on the stand side, there is effect of resistance.

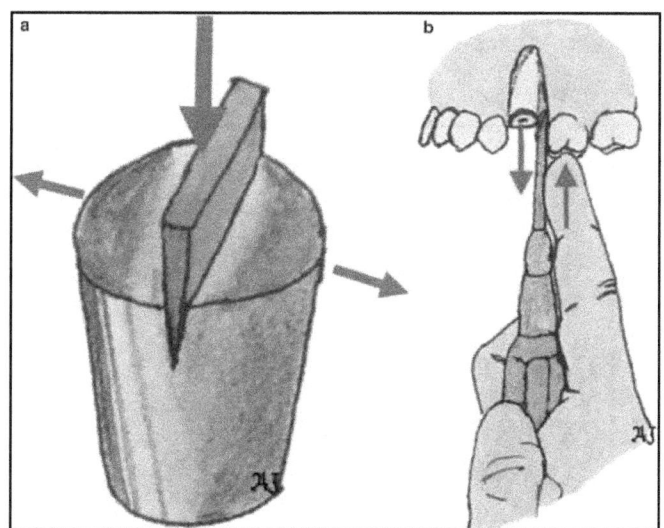

Question - What is the relation between wedge angle and effort to a given resistance?

Answer - The sharper the angle of the wedge the less effort required to make it overcome a given resistance.

Note: It depends on resistance, effort, length and height Effort x Length = Resistance x Height

Where,

    Length is 10 mm

    Height is 4 mm

    Resistance = 10

Mechanical advantage is 2.5

Example apexo elevator, cryer's elevator

Apexo elevator displaces the root toward the occlusal plane and therefore out of the socket.

- Wedge elevator is forced between the root and bone parallel to the long axis of the tooth.

Note: Excessive force should be avoided.

Question - The mechanical advantage obtained from the wheel and axle principle is :-

Answer - 4.6

Question - Apex elevator utilizes which principle ?

Answer - Wedge Principle

Question - Mainly elevators in exodontia works on the principle of and fulcrum is between the effort and resistance. In order to gain mechanical advantage the effort arm must be longer than the resistance arm.

Wheel and axle Principle

- This is the modification of lever. There is an effort when applied to the wheel circumference it turns the axle so as to raise a weight.

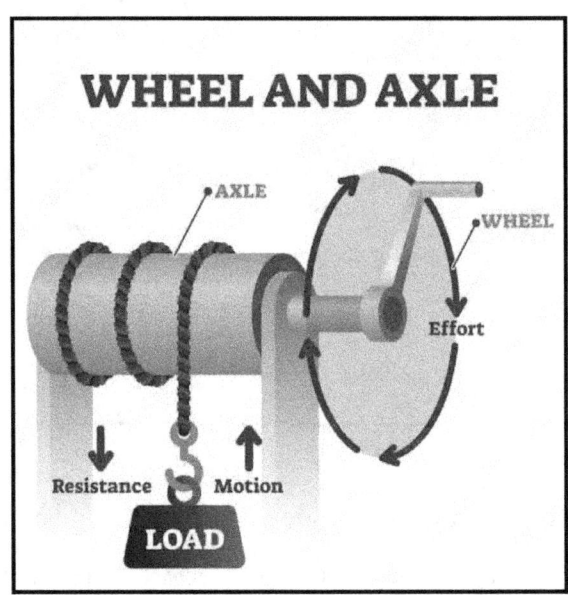

Example Cross bar elevator

Note: It can cause most trauma that fracture the mandible

Effort x radius of wheel = Resistance x radius of axel

R_w – Radius of wheel

R_a – Radius of axel

Where, R_w = 42

R_a = 9

R_w/R_a = 42/9 = 4.6

Mechanical advantage is 4.6

Post extraction care:

- Remove the debris from the socket if needed
- Curattage should be done for peri apical lesion/ pathology if visible radio graphically

- Any tooth fragments or bone chip should be removed
- Compress the bucco lingual plates to their original configuration
- Sharp edges of bone to be smoothed with the help of bone rounder and bone file.
- To control the hemorrhage, a moistened gauze piece should be kept over the socket, so that it fits into the space.

Question - What is the importance of compression after extraction ?

Answer - It is important because it reduce any expansion of the buccal or lingual, labial or lingual buccopalatal or labiopalatal alveolar plate resulting from the extraction process thereby reducing size at helps in healthy.

- Also to reduce the volume of residual blood clot within the socket and helps in healing.

Instructions to the patients:

Bleeding: The wet gauze pack to be held between the jaws in the extraction site for 30 to 45 minutes

- Forceful spitting can be the cause of bleeding, so for 24 hour no forceful spitting should be carried out
- Restrict the excessive physical activity.

Swelling: Application of ice cap / ice cube / ice pack for first day only briefly and intermittently
- Reach its maximum until 48 to 72 hour post operatively

Diet: Soft diet and cold diet is advisable for first 24 hour after extraction.
- Chew on side opposite to that of surgery
- Do not chew the food which is difficult to masticate

Question - Why should one avoid carbonated drinks after tooth extraction ?

Answer - The carbonated bubbles in soda can dislodge the blood clot needed to heal, making recovery process longer and more painful. (Do not take for 4 days)

Note: Water, juice, milk, Gatorade / powerage are the best to take after extraction.

- Smoking is contraindicated after tooth extraction because it increase the level of pain to the extraction site, dislodge the formation of clot, hamper the healing process.

Hygiene: Mouth wash to be avoided for 24 hours after extraction
- Rinse the mouth with warm saline and one tea spoon of salt
- Do not clean the teeth with routine tooth brush
- Clean the extraction socket if food debris stucks

Question - How does warm salt water help after tooth extraction ?

Answer - Salt kills bacteria of oral cavity because it increases the PH levels in the mouth, salt prevents infection by rinsing away plague and debris from the site. It acts on principal of osmosis.

Pain: Prescribed medications to be taken to reduce pain within 45 minutes of extraction. This will avoid the medication to take effect before the effect of anesthesia is worn off.

Note: To prevent stiffness and to stimulate circulation jaw exercises may be done.

Sleeping posture: Patients are instructed not to sleep on the side of extraction (Right side or left side) for 24 hours because doing this there are chances of dislodgement of clot from the extraction side since pressure is create there.

Note: Central hemangioma is an absolute contraindication for extraction of teeth doing this results in profuse bleeding and death of patient.

- The best time of extraction in pregnancy is second trimester. (The first trimester is the stage of organo genesis of foetus and the foetus is highly susceptible to developmental malformations if the mother passes through stress and pain. In third trimester large quantities of hormones are released into blood. The pituitary gland secrets oxytocin which stimulate uterine contractions and hence there is chance of premature labour.

Exodontia Procedure: (Simple extraction)

Commonly used instrument in extraction procedure is forceps. Mostly erupted teeth are used to extract.

Question - Where should the tip of the dental forcep be grasped on a tooth ?

Answer - To the root of a tooth and exert force directly to the root mass to displace from the socket.

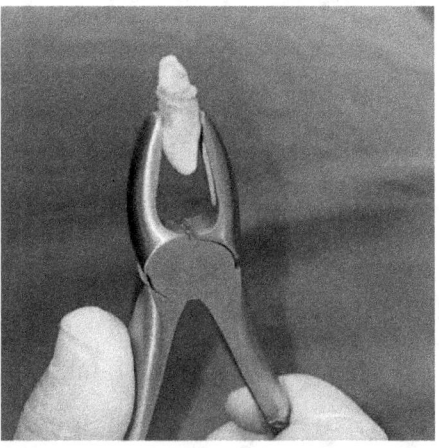

Question - Is the heavy force matter in tooth extraction or fitness/ movement or/ controlled force ?

Answer - Fitness/ movement and controlled force matters the most while extracting the teeth. Excessive force may injure local tissues and can destroy surrounding bone and tooth.

Question - Rotatory movement is used for the extraction of :-

(a) Maxillary lateral incisor   (b) Maxillary central incisor

(c) Mandibular canine   (d) All of the above

Answer - b

Question - Which position should a patient be kept if a pregnant patient falls into syncope during extraction?

Answer - In left lateral position because to avoid pressure on inferior vena cava by fetus, which results in poor venous return and hypotension. The patient is turned onto left side to relieve the pressure.

Intra Alveolar Extraction

FORCEPS USE:

Forceps are used to grasp the roots of teeth?

Note: Forceps are not used to grasp the crown of teeth. The blades of forcep is designed to cover the root circumference.

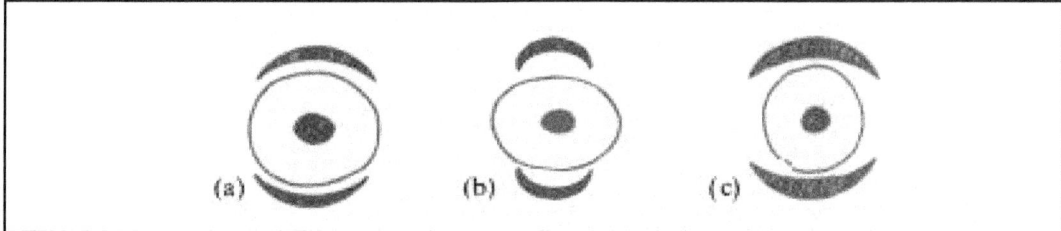

(a) Forcep blades with curvature ideal to fit evenly around the circumference of the root. (b) Two point contact of forceps blades on either side of the root. (c) Single point contact on each side of the root.

Note: The tips of forceps should be pointed so as it penetrates into the periodontal fibers between root and surrounding bone.

Question - How can one sharpen the forceps ?

Answer - Forceps can be sharpen using a sand paper disc on the outer aspect of forcep blade. Blunt and thick blade tip may lead to crushing of surrounding tissue. Sharpening stone.

Forceps Used For Extraction Of Teeth:

Note: Upper forceps have their handles in line with the blades. Whereas handles of lower forceps are angulated at 90^0 to the blades.

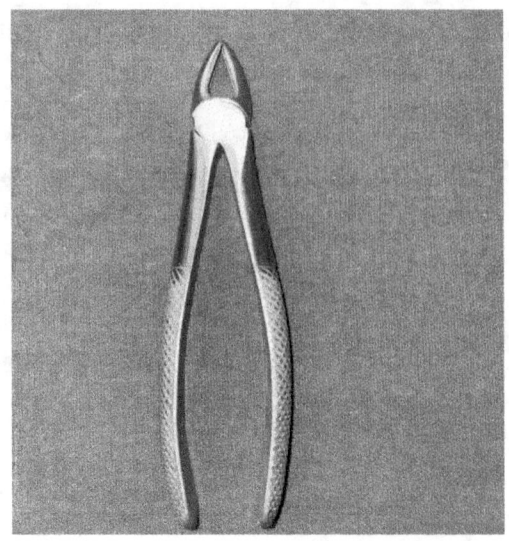

Straight Forcep (for maxillary anterior teeth)

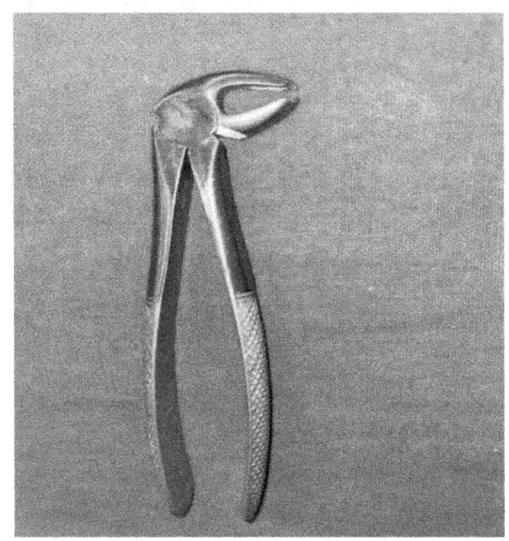

Forcep angulated at 90^0 (for mandibular teeth)

- Simplest design
- Suitable for Central incisor, Lateral incisor & canine
- Most efficient pattern of dental forcep is the upper straight forcep

Note: Blades and handles united by a hinge joint.

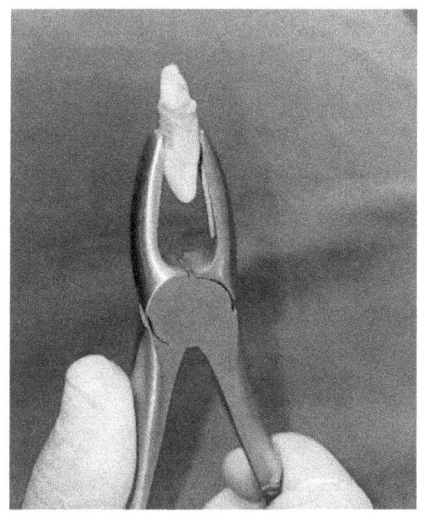

Grasping of upper anterior forceps

Question - Why the forceps blades should have two point contact and not one point contact ?

Answer - Forceps blades with one point contact will probably be crushed when it is gripped.

Maxillary Teeth Extraction

Central Incisor/ Lateral Incisor: The labial side of alveolar bone is thinner than palatal bone. So the first movement is towards the labial side of bone than palatal force is applied. Rotational force/ movement can be applied on central incisor but should be minimized for lateral incisor.

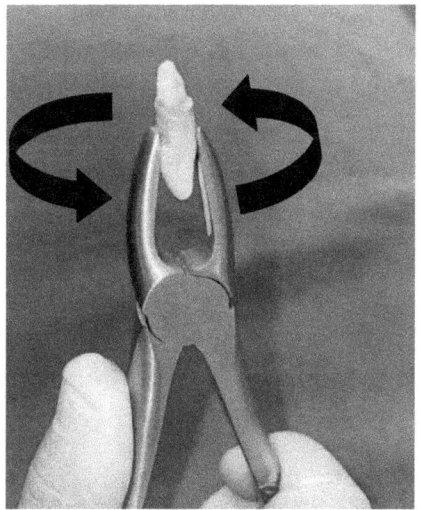

Application of rotational forces

Question - Why rotational force should not be given on upper lateral incisor ?

Answer - Rotational force should not be applied on upper lateral incisor because the root is flat mesiodistally and a groove is present on lateral incisor. While rotating there may be chances of breakage of root.

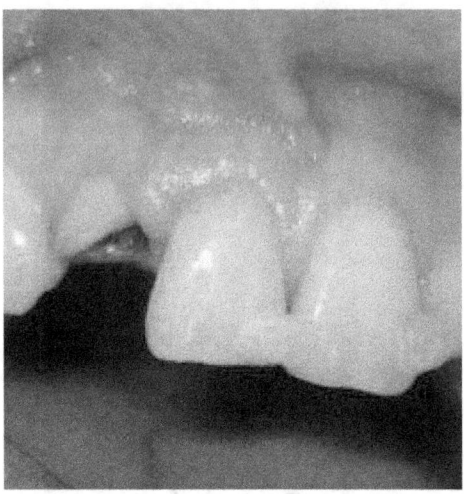

Fracture of upper lateral incisor during application of rotational force.

Maxillary Canine:

This tooth is the longest tooth in the mouth. The bone over the labial aspect of maxillary canine is usually thin. The extraction in difficult because it has long root.

Question - Why the labial bone of maxillary canine is thin ?

Answer - Because it produces a bulge on the anterior surface of maxilla called canine eminence.

To grasp the maxillary canine, one should hold the tooth as apical as possible. The direction of movement of forcep initially is buccal direction followed by palatal movement. A rotational force may be used in expanding the tooth socket. When adjacent teeth are missing or extracted. Once the tooth has been luxated, it is delivered from the socket in a labial incisal direction with labial fractional forces. While luxating the operator feels a portion of labial bone fracture.

Note: If palpating digits indicates that small amount of bone has fractured and is attached to the canine tooth, continue the extraction in usual manner.

If palpating digits indicates that large amount/ portion of labial bone has fractured the operation should the surgical procedure immediately. The operator should raise the mucosa over the fractured bone with the help of periosteal elevator. With the help of forceps free the fractured bone from the tooth with periosteal elevator as a lever to separate the bone from tooth root.

- If the bone gets detached from the periosteum during extraction it should be removed.

Question - Why the detached bone should be removed ?

Answer - It should be removed because it is most likely non vital and may actually prolong wound healing.

Maxillary First Premolar

Maxillary first premolar teeth has two roots. The roots are bifurcated in one third to one half. More prone to fracture specially in older person/ patient in whom the density of bone is great and elasticity of bone is small. While using pre molar forcep. Initial movement should be buccal and while giving palatal movement a controlled and small amounts of force should be applied to prevent fracture of palatal root tip.

Note: When the tooth is luxated buccally, the more chances of breaking root is the labial root.

When the tooth is luxated palatally then more chances of breaking root is the palatal root.

Question - Why the labial root is easier to retrieve compared to palatal root ?

Answer - Labial root is easier to retrieve because of the thin overlying bone. Therefore, buccal pressure should be greater than palatal pressure.

- Rotational force should be avoided
- Buccal and fractional forces are used to extract the teeth from the socket and that too in occlusal direction

Maxillary Second Premolar:

- It is a single rooted tooth fractures rarely. Thin buccal plate and thick palatal alveolar palate.
- Forces used to extract maxillary second premolar is firstly buccal movement, than palatal movement than buccal occlusal direction with rotational and fractional force.

Maxillary Molar:

- They are having three roots.
- Both buccal roots are close to each other while the palatal root is widely diverges towards the palate.
- Like other maxillary teeth the buccal cortical plate is thin whereas the palatal bone is thick.

Note: If the sinus is in close proximity to the roots and widely diverged then there is a chances of increased likelihood of sinus perforation if trying removal of a portion of the sinus floor during tooth removal.

Question - Where should be the tip projection of upper molar forcep ?

Answer - Tip projection on the buccal beaks to fit into the buccal bifurcation.

- Cow horn forceps are used if there is large crown caries or restoration.
- Heavy forces required to extract the molar teeth in buccal and palatal movement and Avoid Rotationalforces because it is multi rooted.
- It is preferable to fracture a buccal root than a palatal roots.
- One must minimize palatal force since this is the force that fracture the palatal root.

Maxillary Second Molar: Similar to that of maxillary first molar except that the roots tend to be shorter and less divergent with the buccal roots more commonly fused into a single root. Extraction is same as of maxillary first molar.

Maxillary Third Molar:
- It has conical roots
- It is easily removed
- Buccal bone is thin and the roots are usually fused and conical
- Extraction can be done with the elevator alone.

Mandibular Anterior Teeth:
- Mandibular canine is longer than mandibular incisor and heavier also
- The chances of fracture of mandibular incisors are more if adequate pre-extraction luxation is not done
- The chances of fracture of labial and lingual cortical bone is more in incisor extraction because these bones are thin enough.
- The forces during extraction of mandibular anterior teeth should be in labial and lingual direction with equal pressure both ways once the tooth is mobile rotational movement may be used frictional forces are applied in labio incisor direction.

Stobie's Technique:

This technique simply states that is multiple anterior teeth is indicated straight elevator is inserted both the lower incisors and rotated. Doing this technique the teeth will loosen both the adjacent and facilitate the extraction.

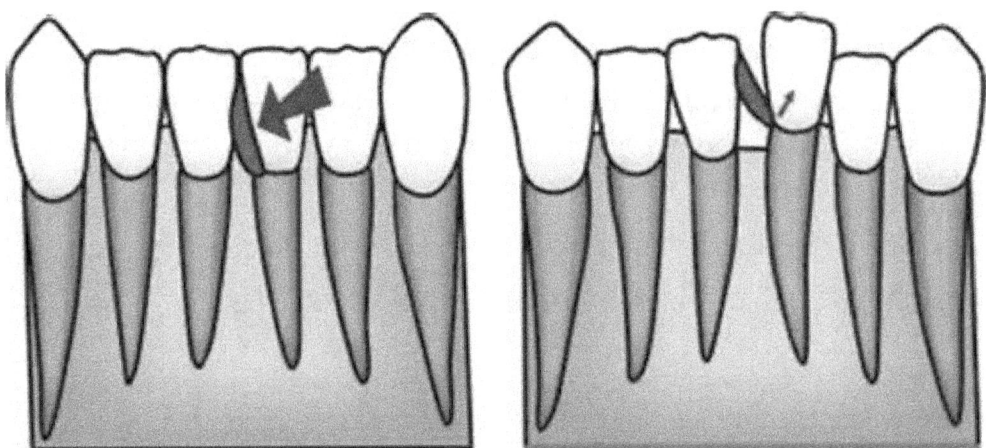

Stobie technique, A, A straight elevator is inserted between lower incisors and rotated. B, Both teeth are loosened and the extraction of them with forceps is facilitated.

Mandibular Premolars:
- Easy to remove premolar because the roots tend to be straight and conical sometimes slender
- The labial aspect of bone is thin whereas the lingual bone is heavier.
- Lower premolar forcep is used to extract the premolar

- The basic movement is used during extraction of premolar is bucco-lingual direction and finally rotational movement is used and get the tooth out in occusal buccal direction.

Mandibular Molars:

- These tooth usually have two roots
- Roots of mandibular first molar are widely divergent than those of the mandibular second molar
- Roots are heavy and strong
- The overlying alveolar bone is heavier than the bone on any other teeth
- Mandibular molar forceps are used for extraction of the mandibular molar
- Strong apical pressure is applied to set the beaks of the forceps apically as far as possible
- Strong buccal and lingual motion is then used to expand the socket
- Get the tooth out of socket in bucco occusal direction
- The lingual alveolar bone of mandibular second molar is more thin than mandibular first molar so it is easier to extract the mandibular second molar lingually than buccal pressure.
- Cow horn of mandibular tooth is used while the root of molar are clearly bifurcated. Squeezing the beaks of the forceps into the bifurcation. Buccal and lingual movements used to expand the socket.

Note: Care must be taken with these forceps to prevent damaging the opposite arch (maxillary teeth) since lower molar may actually pop out of socket and thus release the forceps to strike the upper teeth.

- The third molar is delivered in the lingual occusal direction

The Correct Way Of Forceps Application

Forceps blades are applied to the buccal and lingual surface of keeping in mind the long axis either on or parallel to that of the tooth.

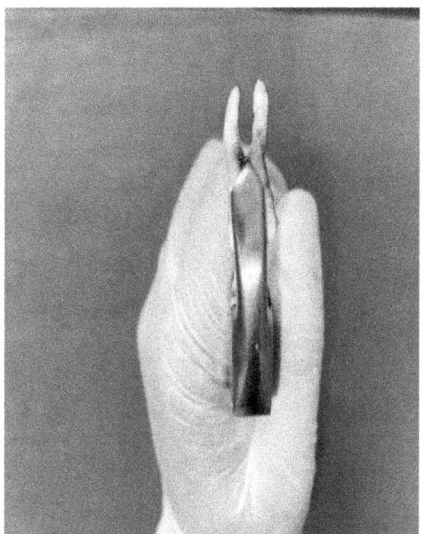 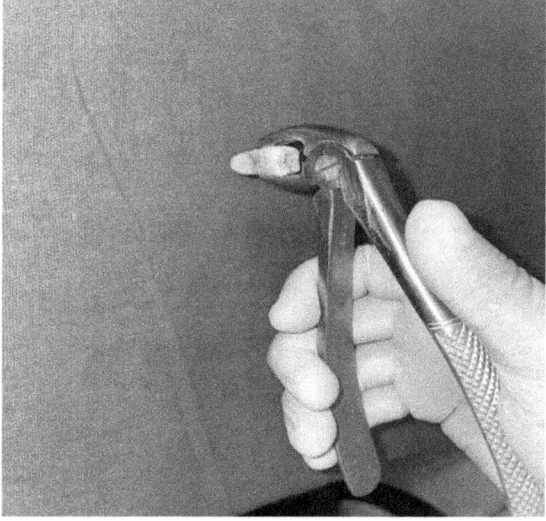

Beaks are in long axis of tooth

The beak of forcep blades are inserted through the periodontal membrane between the investing alveolar bone and root surface to towards the apex. Left little finger is used to engage the blade of forcep in the periodontal membrane.

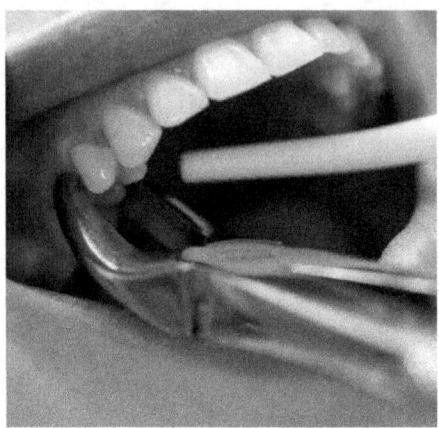 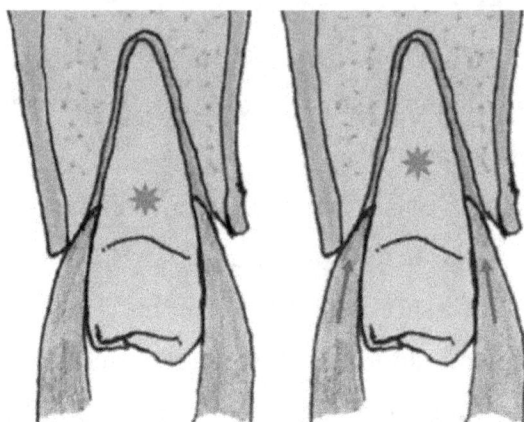

Beak of forcep blade inserted through the periodontal membrane

Note: If there is cervical caries on the buccal or lingual surface of tooth. The movement of forcep during extraction should be applied to the carious side first. Doing this can reduce the risk of fracture of the tooth.

- Operator should move his/her trunk from the hips and not by moving his/her elbow. While extracting the teeth.

During extraction bucco lingual and linguo buccal movements are made. When the tooth is felt to loosen from the socket and begin to rise out of its socket than rotatory or figure of eight movements should be given.

Question - Why after extraction expanded socket is compressed?

Answer - After extraction expanded socket is compressed to reduce the distortion of both soft and hard tissue support.

Note: Only maxillary central incisor and mandibular second premolar have straight conical roots and primary rotational movement can be given.

- A spiral fracture of tooth root many occur is rotatory movement is continued.

Errors Encountered During Forcep Extraction:

i) Incorrect alignment of the forceps blade

ii) Griping the crown:- Griping the crown with forcep blades leads to fracture of crown specially when the tooth is restored or carious.

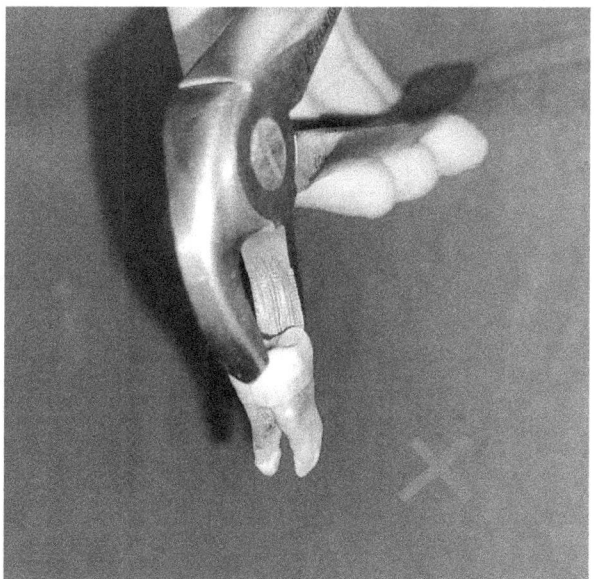

Gripping the crown

iii) Failure to grip the root:- Loss of maintaining firm pressure dependent upon the forceps handle being held firmly together. Failure to achieve this may leads to fracture of tooth.

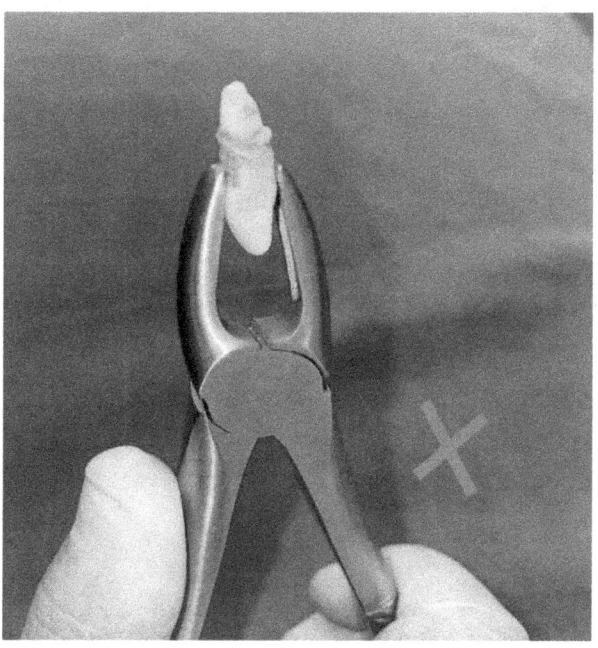

Removal of Deciduous teeth: Movement that should be applied during removal of deciduous teeth is buccal and forward rotation. If in case the root fragments in broken better to leave the small root fragments in the socket.

Question - Why is it advised to leave the small root fragments in the extraction socket while it breaks?

Answer - It is advised to leave the small root fragments in the extraction socket because there is chances to damage or displace the permanent successor in attempts to locate and remove it. With time the root fragments will undergo resorption or exfoliation.

Note: If attempting to remove the root fragments the soft tissue must be reflected adequately so that the operator can see the exact relationship of the permanent successor and enable the operator to deliver the root fragment under direct vision.

Operator Positioning:

For all upper teeth and those in the lower left quadrant, best position to stand is in front of the patient.

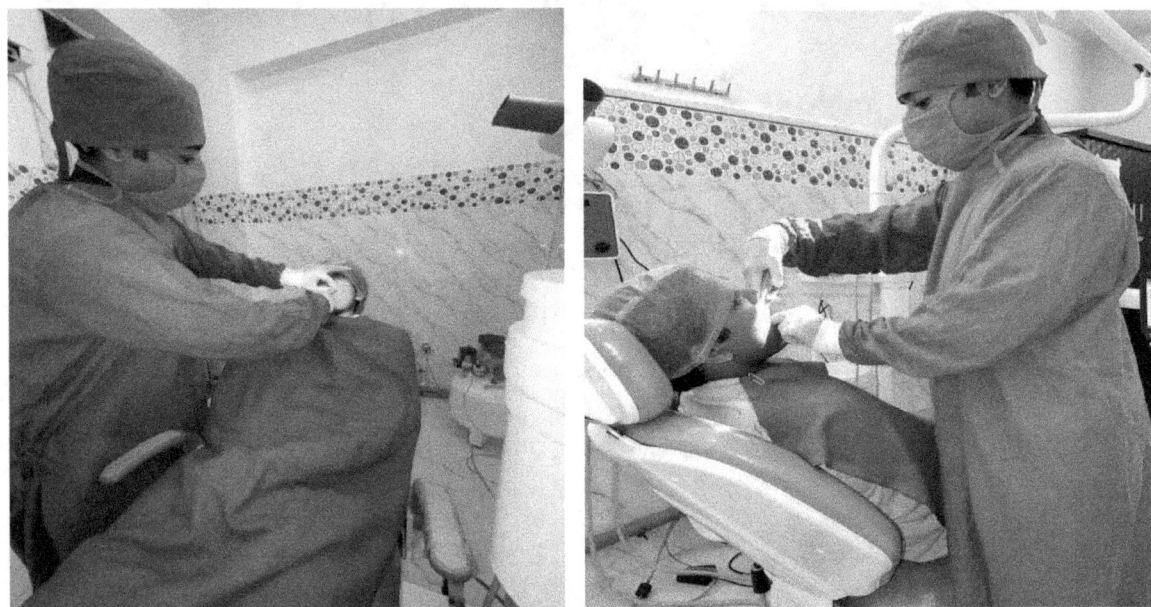

For extraction of lower right quadrant the best position to stand is slightly behind the patient. (at 11 o'clock position).

- Consider the dental chair as a clock face with the head at 12 o'clock. Both upper quadrants can be approached at 7 o'clock position.

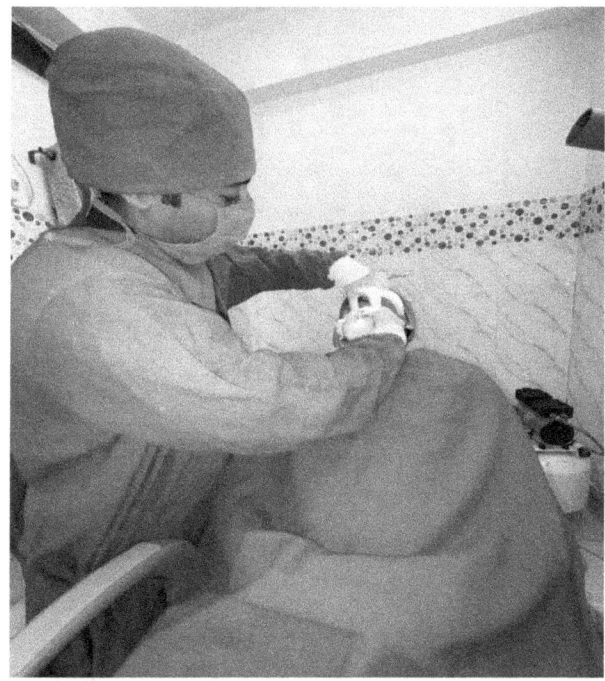

- The lower left anterior teeth is reached at 10 o'clock position.

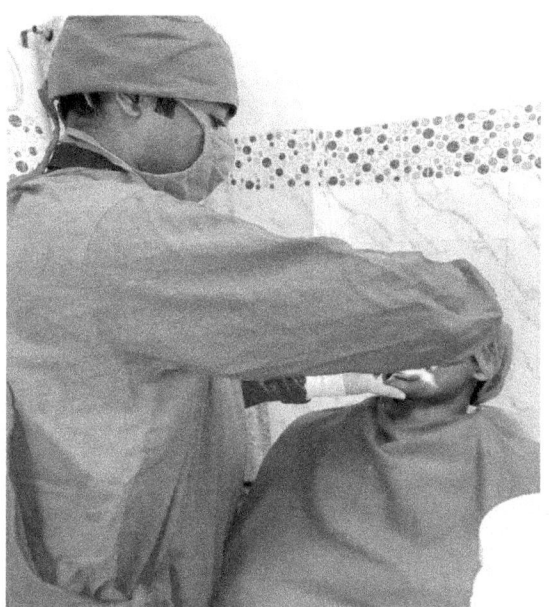

- The lower left posterior teeth can be approached at 7 o'clock position.
- Assistant sit to patient's left at 4 o'clock position.

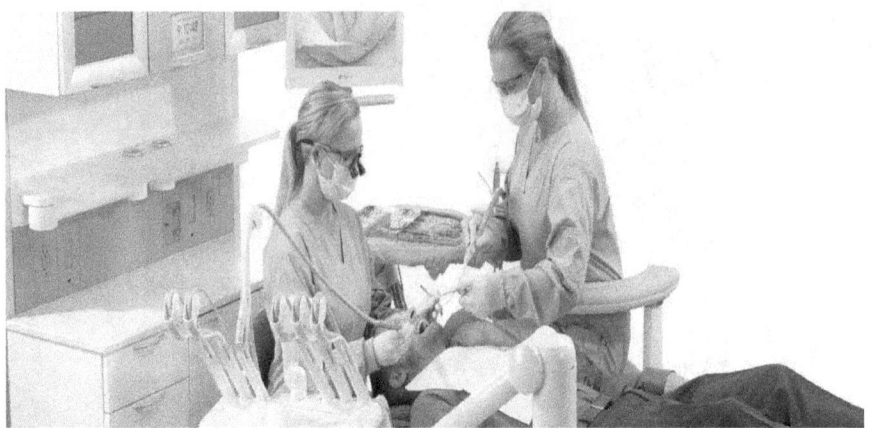

Forceps Grip:

The handle ends should be against the heel of the hand so that pressure generated along the long axis of the instrument to the tooth is powerful and good secure.

Note: The thumb finger of right hand should be placed just below the hinge and used to adjust the width of the blades as the handles are gently squeeze together or moved apart by the fingers.

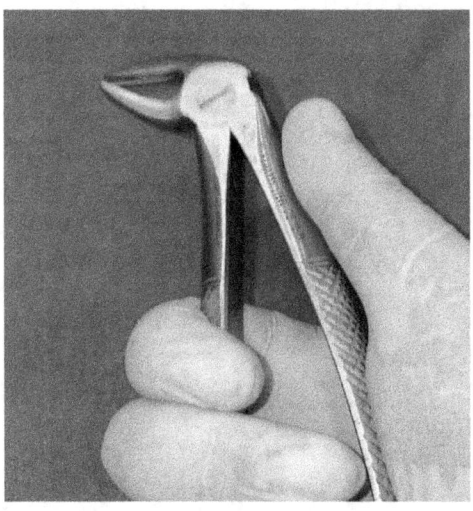

- The use of little finger inside the handles is to widen the handles as the forceps are adjusted while extraction of a tooth.

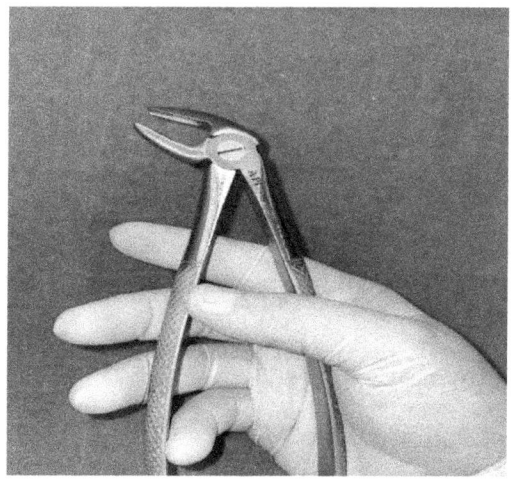

The little finger should be moved outside the handles

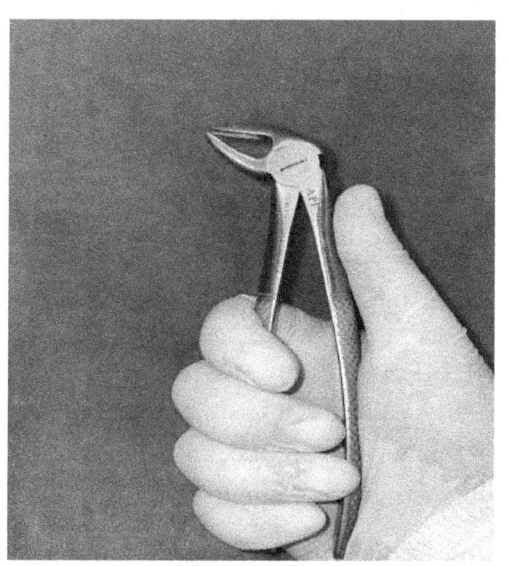

As the tooth is gripped

Table: Direction of movement for maxillary teeth

Tooth in Maxilla	Root pattern	Movement
3rd Molar	Roots are variable	Buccal disto- buccal twist
2nd Molar	Normally three roots as for first molar	Buccal disto- buccal twist
1st Molar	Two thin buccal roots one strong palatal root three roots diverge markedly	Buccal – predominantly disto-buccal twist to deliver
2nd Premolar	One generally strong root	Buccal
1st Premolar	Two thin roots very fragile	Wiggle and pull only

	Buccal + Palatal	
Canine	Long thick root triangular cross section	Buccal
Lateral Incisor	Oval cross section Flattened mesio-distally	Buccal + gentle rotation
Central Incisor	Conical or circular cross section	Rotation

Table: Directions of movement for mandibular teeth

Tooth in Mandible	Root Pattern	Movement
Third Molar	Root pattern very variable	Lingual figure of 8
2nd Molar	Normally as for 1st molar	Lingual buccal figure of 8
1st Molar	Two mesial roots on distal	Bucco lingual figure of 8
First and second Premolars-Round cross section		Rotation

Canine Long thick root –triangular cross section

Central + lateral incisors-thin oval cross-section ,flattened mesiodistally.

Extracting Deciduous Teeth:

Deciduous teeth have less substantial roots that are often significantly resorbed. But because of having small mouth of pediatric patient is sometime difficult to remove molars and canine teeth. Premolars are enclosed within the roots of their deciduous predecessors and there will be chances to damage the permanent teeth when the deciduous teeth are being extracted further.

Note: The fractured remnants of root during extraction of deciduous roots may be advisable to leave the root fragments to be shed or resorb naturally instead to risk damage to the permanent successor.

One should keep in mind when applying forcep blades. It goes down the periodontal membranes and engages the roots. Lingual movement causes the tooth to rise from the socket.

Handling Elevators:

An elevator applies force between the tooth and the surrounding bone. Forceps exert more directional control on the tooth than elevators, therefore be less likely to fracture and tends to move long its own path of withdrawal and therefore less chances of fracture. Elevators acts as wedge with one side acting the force on the tooth and other side acting the force in the adjacent bone which is called fulcrum.

Thick wedge will not gain access to thin space and too wide the tip will merely jam at the first rotatory movement. The narrow tip will rotate round and round in a large space correct sized elevator will enable the displacement of a root without much lateral force.

Question - It is permissible for an adjacent tooth to be used as a fulcrum ?

Answer - Yes, it is permissible for an adjacent tooth to be used as a fulcrum only if that tooth is also to be extracted at the same time otherwise the fulcrum for elevation should always be on bone.

Note: Engaging the elevator inter proximally quadrant between first molar and second premolar of the same quadrant and trying to extract the first molar keep in mind the equal and opposite force on the second premolar may be enough to cause fracture of the tooth or may displace from the socket.

Positioning Of Elevators:

Same like forceps, the blade of the elevator or the tip of the elevator can gain access to the surface of root the force applying on the elevator should fall parallel to the long axis of instrument and the index finger should rest on shaft towards the tip of elevator. The remaining four finger grasp the handle and provide the rotational force.

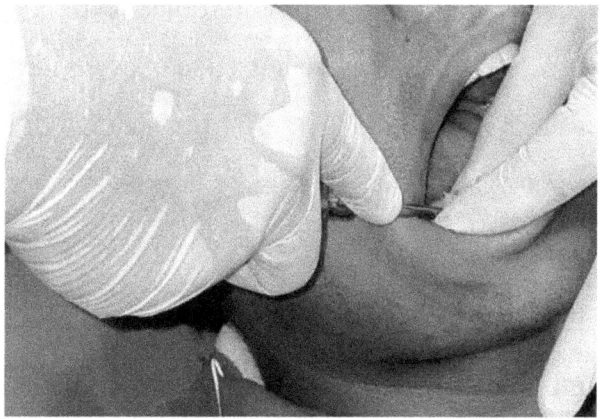

Note: Elevators should never be used as class I levers

Note: Apply the elevator from the buccal aspect in upward and lingual direction if the root of the tooth is straight and control.

- Apply the force from the mesial aspect of root if the tooth root curvature is pointed distally.

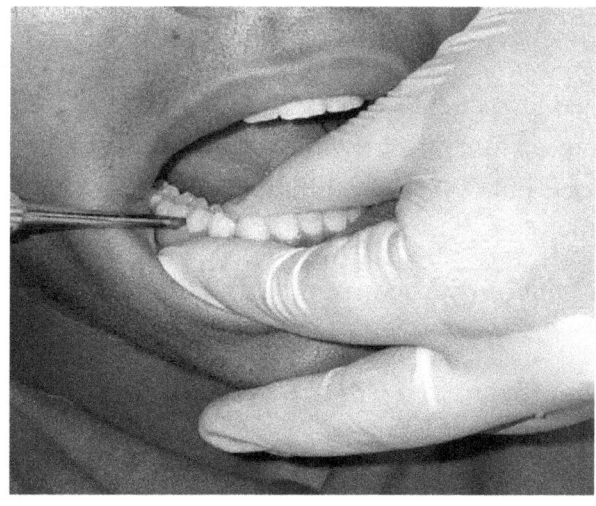

- Apply the force from the distal aspect of root if the tooth root curvature is pointed mesially.

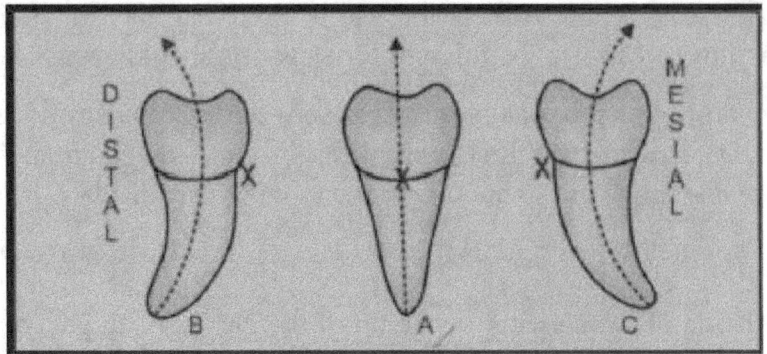

- If the distal bone is present on mandibular third molar than mesial force is contraindicated.

- Make a buccal purchasing point for an elevator on the buccal surface of root at an angle of 45 degree to the long axis of root only when the root is fused or multi rooted teeth.

Note: Because of high blood pressure reactionary haemorrhage occurs after extraction.

- Primary haemorrhage occurs as a normal path of surgery from a unavoidable trauma during extraction.

- Intermediate or reactionary haemorrhage occurs within 24 hours. Post operatively or due to rise in BP or slipping of ligature.

- Secondary hemorrhage occurs 7-14 days post operatively and occurs as a result of breakdown of the clot on account of infection.

Note: Displacement of a root into the maxillary sinus during extraction is most likely to happen during the extraction of maxillary first molar. Usually the palatal root of maxillary 1st molar is present closer to maxillary sinus followed by 2nd premolar 1st premolar and last the maxillary second molar.

Question - A patient who is on dicoumoral therapy require a tooth extraction. Which laboratory test is the most valuable in evaluating this patient's surgical risk ?

(a) Complete blood cell count   (b) Prothrombin time

(c) Clotting time   (d) Bleeding time

Answer - b

Prothrombine time is increased in patients o anticoagulant therapy or salicylate therapy. It is also prolonged in case of liver distances in deficiently of factor I, II, V, VII & X. Normal prothrombin is 11-15 sec. Extraction can be carried out. When prothrombin time within 1 1/2 times the normal prothrombin time i.e., about 20-23 sec.

Question - A male is taking 60 mg of hydrocortisone daily. On the day before extraction this dose should be :-

(a) Remain unchanged   (b) Reduced to half   (c) Doubled   (d) Reduced to one fourth

Answer - a

The patients under corticosteroids therapy will have concomitant decreased adrenal reserve and will decompensate when exposed to additional stress. In order to prevent adrenal crisis the dose should not be missed.

Trans Alveolar Extraction:

This type of extraction needs surgical procedure so called as open extraction or surgical extraction.

Indications

Crown: The carious crown heavily restored crown, FPD may need surgical procedure to extract because these factors weakens the teeth and crown may get shattered or crushed when gripped by forceps.

- Roots: Roots like bulbous, multi rooted ankylosed teeth hypercementosis dilacerated divergent or teeth undergone root canal treatment.

- Bulbous roots creates the mechanical obstruction while removal because it cover the large space inside the socket might not be possible for delivery of the root from socket and this tooth need surgical extraction.

- Multi rooted teeth are having individual different long axis and for this reason forces are needed along the long axis of each root and hence need for transalveolar extraction of such tooth.

- Ankylosed teeth are fused to alveolar bone, loss of periodontal ligament. If excess force is applied to remove the teeth, fracture of tooth or alveolar bone will occur.

- Hypercementosis teeth are difficult to remove because of smaller diameter of socket at the cervical level and dense root in the apical region operator need increased forces which may fracture the root or bone.

- Dilacerated roots are having hook like structure while extracting non surgically fracture of apical end may occur because of increased resistance to delivery.

- Divergent roots are seen in maxillary molars frequently. Due to non-parallelism of roots it is difficult to extract tooth in one piece and need surgical extraction.

- Root canal treated teeth are brittle in nature tooth may crush during application of extraction forces and operator need to go for transalveolar extraction.

- Intra alveolar attempt is failed

- Geminated dilacerated tooth

- Heavily restored tooth

- History of attempted extraction

- Retained roots not accessible to forceps

- Hypercementosed teeth

- Ankylosed teeth

- Proximity to vital structures

- Highly carious heavily restored endodontically treated adjacent teeth

- Prosthetic concern when simple extraction cause more bone loss

Main components of trans alveolar extraction are:

A Mucoperiosteal flap design

B Bone removal used to facilitate tooth/root removal

C Deliver the tooth/root from socket

Mucoperiosteal flap design: This is important for clear visible and accessible designing should be such that they provide good visual and mechanical access.

Note: Suture should not be placed over blood clot and avoid the buccal sulcus obliteration

Question - Why suture should not be placed over blood clot ?

Answer - Suture should not be placed over blood clot because it promotes the microorganism to grow over there and causes breakdown of wound

Principles of flap design:

Incision:

Using no 15 blade the incision should be made on gingiva down to break full thickness flap elevated it by periosteal elevator

Envelope flaps: An incision along the crest of mandibular edentulous ridge will permit the buccal and lingual mucoperiosteal flaps to be raised.

Shape Of Flaps:

It is raised that have two or three sides and in some situation only one side along the gingival margin this provide restricted access to the crest of bone. This can get at the risk of stretching and tearing the soft tissues as they are undermined with the help of persisted elevator.

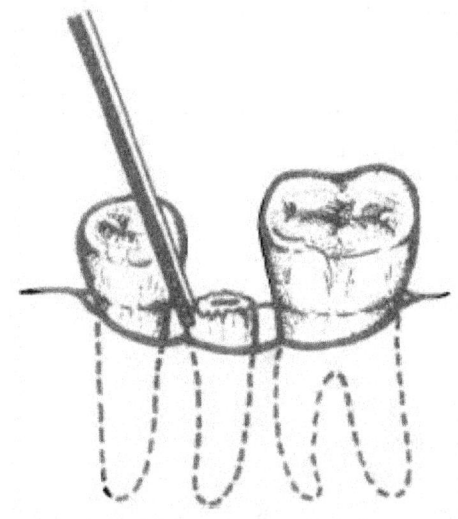

(a) An incision only along the gingival margin allows very limited access to the superficial part of a root fractured at crestal bone level.

Two – sided flaps:

This is made along the gingival margin with single incision called as relieving incision make and angled incision obliquely to the attached buccal gingival gingival into vestibular mucosa. This type of flap provides good access for transalveolar extractions.

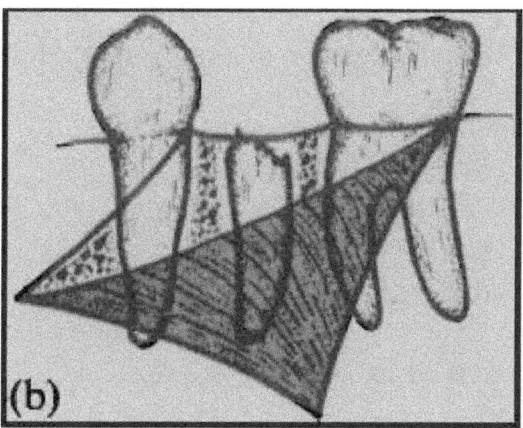

(b) Two-sided flap with a mesial relieving incision-this design of flap provides adequate access for most trans-alveolar extractions.

Three- sided flaps: in three sided flap. We give a relieving incision at the distal aspect of flap. This provide more exposure of the underlying bone & root of teeth and allows extra mobilization of the soft tissues.

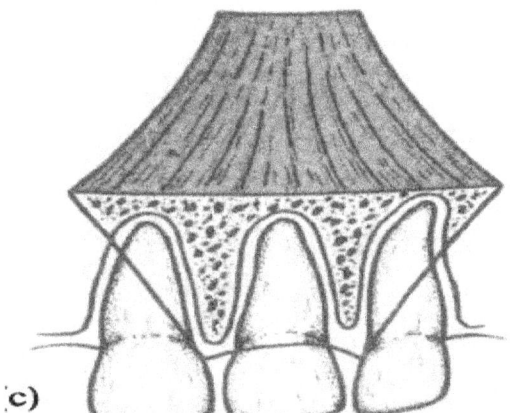

(c) Three –sided flap with mesial and distal relieving incisions –this flap improves the access to the apices of teeth.

Indication of three- sided flaps used during apicoectomy oro antral fistula

Accessibility – flaps should be large enough to permit good and clear access to the working site without the need of stretching and tearing risk of soft tissue.

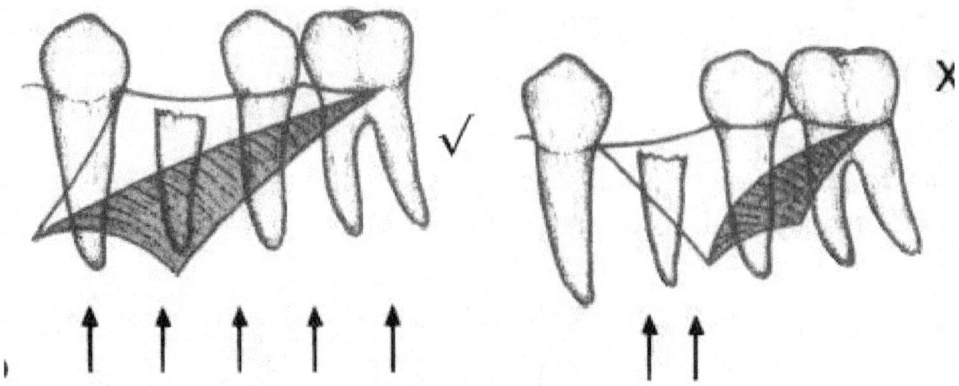

(a) Correct design of flap with a broad base.(b) Poor flap with narrow base, so restricting blood supply to the flap and limiting access to the buried root.

Incisions making;

Use 15 no. blade with firm pressure on soft tissue so that all the layers are divided in a single stroke the incision line should be single and clean secondary or second cut on the incision line may delay healing because few ragged margins can be seen and also difficult to suture.

Note:- relieving incisions should reach the vestibular mucosa and this allow the flap to be mobilized easily

Do not over extent the incision deep into the sulcus because this may cause hemorrhage from buccinators muscle may damage the mental nerve

The bp blade is held in a pen grasp position directed at the right angle to the surface of soft tissue. Where the vertical incisions need keep in mind the BP blade to be held parallel to the long axis of the tooth and the blade get a good contact along the gingival crevice.

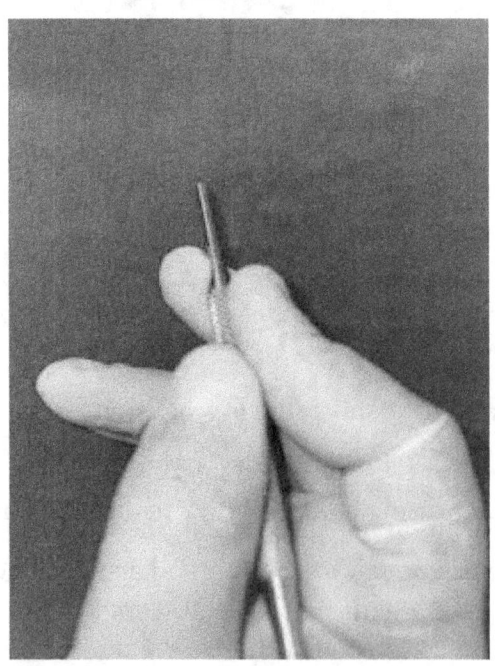

Flap Reflection:

With the help of periosteal elevator, elevate the full thickness flap from the underlying boneNote-

Elevate the mucoperiosteum through the anterior edge of vestibular mucosa and not the attached gingival uncover the bony surface by advancing the elevation of flap do not undermine or tunnel because this may tore or stretched the flap. If these is a resistance while reflecting the flap these are chances that the incision has not divided the periosteum the margin and probable perforation can encounter

Question - what is button holed ?

Answer - where there is chronic periapical infection is present and elevating the flap with the shape of elevator in the sinus of buccal sulcus area may perforate and making the flap liable to button holed at the site.

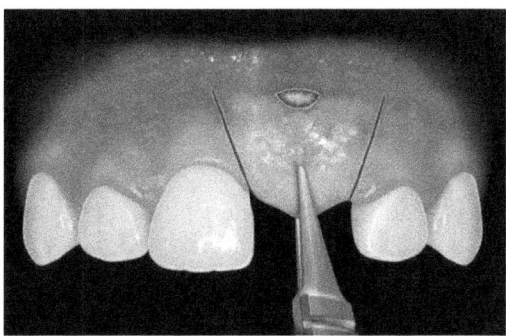

Prevention of flap necrosis:

1. Flap should be wider at base than apex so that it provide adequate blood supply to all over the flap
2. Length should not be more than the width
3. Releasing incisions should converge at free end
4. Flap should not be grasped with sharp instruments and should not be twisted and stretched excessively, doing such might damage the blood supply of flap

Prevention of flap dehiscence:

1. Tensionless suturing to prevent necrosis of the flap margins
2. Handle the tissue gently to maintan the vitality
3. Approximate flap margins over sound and healthy bone

Bone Removal:

Bone is removed

1. To expose the tooth and clear its path of exit
2. To provide suitable point of application of elevator

After extraction dentist need to trim the walls of socket

1. To remove sharp edges and spicules
2. To smooth the ridge contour to assist the prosthetics

Bone can be removed using bone cutting bur (round and straight) using no 701,702,703 in a straight hand piece or using chisels or gouges burs are proffered mostly because of its precise cutting predictably and efficiently. The maxilla bone is more chancellor comfort to mandible and need less force to break away the bone using chisel whereas in mandible requires more force to cut the bone using chisel mallet bone nibbler and rongeur are used to trim the sharp piece of bone and prominent projection

Rotary Cutting Instruments:

Optimum bone cutting at high torque at bur speeds in 1000-3000 revolutions per minute (RPM)

Question - which burs are ideal for cutting bone ?

Answer - tungsten carbide tipped burs designed for surgical use are ideal for cutting bone

Note: stainless steel burs are adequate for bone cutting but they become blunt very quickly and need to be discarded

Blunt burs do not cut effectively they generate abounded heat at the bone surface

Operator need to know while using hand piece:

Continuous copious irrigation should be done with sterile saline out the tip of running bur or the interface of bur and bone

Do not exceed the temperature of bur greater than 10 degree doing this may lead to burn the bone and can cause necrosis of bone

Secondary fluid irrigation is to be done to wash away bony debris and clogged blood from the operative field this helps to maintain clear visual access

Irrigants that can be used for irrigation is normal saline or betadine mixed with saline

Airoter should not be used to cut the bone a mixture of air and water under high pressure are inappropriate for surgical use as they may force air under the flap and tissue causing surgical emphysema

Bone can be removed with two technique

1. Using the bur shave down the surface of bone with the bur size 8-12 round or fissure pattern.
2. A block of bone piece is dislodge by outlining using a smaller bur.

Other name of round bur is "rosehead burs"

-round bur have less tendency to clog with particles of bone comparatively fissure burs

-difficult to control the lateral cuts

-difficult to judge the cutting depth one buried in bone fissure burs

- lateral cutting is very precisely and clear
- comparatively round bur, fissured bur are less good at drilling penetrating notes

Operator has a grater feel in distinguishing the difference in hardness between bone and dentine

-Bur no 6 is a good choice for guttering.

Widely divergent root, because of multi root teeth it has different path of withdrawal. Tooth become easy to extract wham the crown get separated and the roots get divided with fissured bur with the help of croplands elevator no 1 the individual roots are dispatched each along its own path of withdrawal.

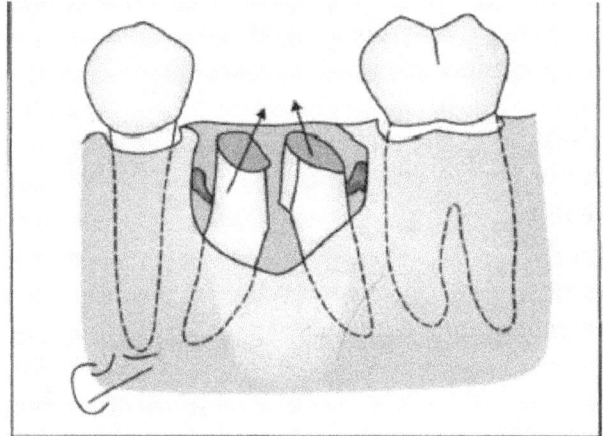

Using chiesel : this technique is used to split the tooth with an osteotome. It has bevel on both sides of its cutting tip. This technique work more faster than bur.

Disadvantage:

The tooth may not split along the intended line

This technique is little sensitive

No space / gap available for instrumentation or movement between the separated fragments

In some cases, the best position to grasp the tooth with the help of forceps is by its crown so sometimes sectioning the crown can make removal of root even more difficult in distoangular inclined third molar or the second premolar or canine in the palatal aspect

Root elevation : preferably sometimes fine bladed forceps are used to reach the root

It is better to leave a small piece of root behind so as to protect the nearby

structures. Note: leave the root fragments in the socket if it is <5 mm

-in attempted extraction if the root becomes non vital or dislodged from the socket, that tooth ideally should be removed as they may be cause for infection.

Sometimes it is difficult to elevate the root upwards so when forcing tooth to come out buccally we need to engage the elevator on the root mass where we made a notch (buccally) the angulations of notch ideally be 45 degree vertically made with round bur

Extraction socket: also known as socket toilet in case if bony prominence is seen should remove with the help of bone rongeur and bone file or with vulcanite bur the margins should be smooth and clear the infracted granules and debris should be removed with help of curette

Socket closure:

The terms used for socket closure is suturing the purpose is to approximate the soft tissue over the bony socket so that the mucoperisteal flap comes in its former position, doing this, it prevents the deposition of food debris in the socket and prevents from contamination it also arrest bleeding and closes the oro antral fistula if hampered by chance

Note: hemophilic patients and patient under coverage of bisphosphonate are treated by rubber band and extraction procedure

Question - what is rubber band extraction ?

Answer - the dentist simply place a rubber band around the tooth to be extracted because of the shape of the teeth the rubber band slowly worked its way up or down the sides of the tooth roots destroying the bone and soft tissues and the tooth

Just fall out in about 4 to 6 weeks.

Technological advancement in extraction techniques:

-physics forceps

-Orthodontic extraction

-Lasses

- coronectomy

- piezosurgery

- powered periotome

Physics forceps:

The physics forceps use first class level mechanics to atraumatically extract a tooth from its socket one handle of the device is connected to a bumper which acts as a fulcrum during the extraction together the break and bumper design acts as a simple first class lever a squeezing motion should not used with these forceps by contrast the handles are actually rotated as one unit using a steady yet gentle rotational force with wrist movement only one the tooth is loosen it may be removed with traditional instruments such as conventional forceps.

Orthodontic extraction:

This technique will be of no value for a tooth that cannot move because of ankylosis this technique should be used only in carefully selected cases in conjunction with an orthodontist being certainly difficult time consuming

Technique for open extraction of multi rooted tooth

Maxillary molars with divergent roots: if crown is intact

-reflect the mucoperiosteal flap

-remove small amount of crestal bone

-expose furcation

-separate mesiobuccal and distobuccal roots from rest of the tooth

-extract crown with palatal root with bucco - occlusal pressure

-palatal root with crown are delivered along long axis of palatal root

-avoid palatal force to prevent root fracture

-elevate buccal roots one by one using straight / cryer elevator. Avoid too much apical force to avoidsinus perforation. Apply maximum force mesiodistally

Crown is missing / fractured

-divide the three roots

- extract them individually

First extract buccal roots, then extract palatal root

Mandible first molar:

1st technique

Envelope flap is reflected

Tooth is sectioned buccolingually

Mesial and distal halves are formed

Sectioned tooth is treated as two single rooted teeth

Luxated with straight elevators and extract with universal for

2nd technique

-if crown lost previously reflect flap

-remove crestal bone

Section the two roots

Extract individually

3rd technique

-triangular flap reflected

-sufficient buccal bone removed to expose bifurcation

-mesial root sectioned with burs

-Distal root along with crown extracted

-mesial root elevated with cryers

And not always successful

Laser For Extraction Of Impacted Teeth:

For the surgical extraction of the teeth, the covering bone was first ablated, layer by layer using Er yag laser in the case of fiber-optic Er yag (erbium yttrium – aluminum – granet) laser the fiber is closely guided around the teeth, creating a narrow gap with minimum bone loss the benefit of laser therapy include the creation of a bloodless surgical field and thus improved visualization during surgery decreased post operative pain and limited scaring and contraction time consuming sound and smell significantly inhibition the laser cutting because of overall volume of irrigation and blood covering the bone surface a potential problem with this technique is soft tissue damage for impingement on the mucosa of the cheek and the gingiva in additional working in this area of the month present great difficulty and the action of masseter muscle leads to cheek compression against the orthodontic appliances this technique will be of no value for a tooth that cannot move because of ankylosis. This ankylosis should be used only in carefully selected cases in conjunction with an orthodontist being certainly difficult time consuming and not always successful.

Powered periotome:

This technique is good because it does precise extraction of toot it preserves bone and gingival architecture one can plan for immediate implant placement mechanism of wedging and severing. It serves the periodontal ligament. The multirooted teeth requires sectioning

Piezosurgery:

Piezosurgery is an innovative bone surgery technique that produces a modulated ultrasonic frequency of 24-29 khz and a micro vibration amplitude between 60 and 200 mm/s. the amplitude of the vibration created allows a very clean and precise surgical cut. It works selectively without harming soft tissue such a nerves and blood vessels even with the accidental contact with the cutting tip the surgical control of the device is effortless compared with rotational bur or oscillating of the instrument. Despite the longer time of the procedure the investigators also noted that the piezoelectric osteotomy reduces postoperative facial swelling and trimness use of piezosurgery device to cut and elevate a precisely defined bone lid on the lateral cortex. On the mandible to provide access to the teeth need extraction or even a lesion that needs to be excised. The bone window is then elevated with the help of curved osteotome. After a visual confirmation of an undamaged inferior alveolar nerve and adjacent tissues, the bone lid is placed back into its original position and fixated with absorbable miniplates.

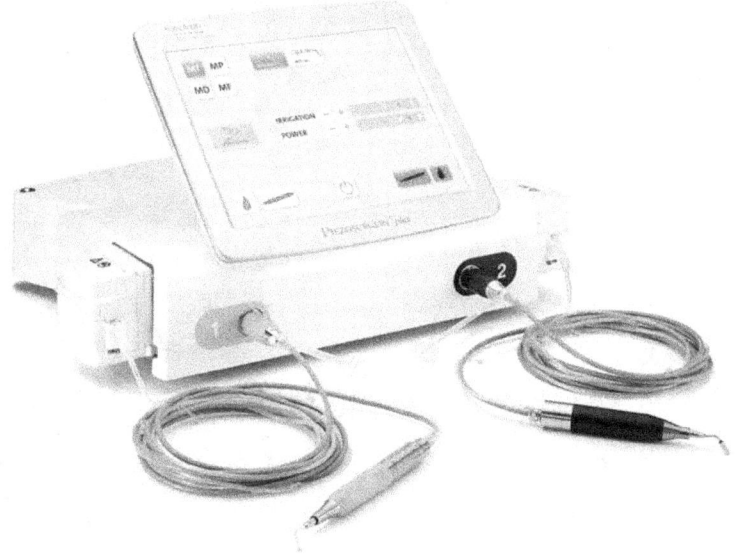

Question - in a patient of liver disease the possible complication during extraction is ?

    a. Dry socket   c. bleeding

    b. Facial space infection   d. loss of clot

Answer - c

Question - dry socket ?
    a. Results from loss of blood clot in the socket
    b. Is treated with reinducing bleeding into the socket
    c. Is a form of osteomyelitis.
    d. Is common in extraction of anterior teeth.

Answer - a

Dry socket is a form of localized osteotitis characterized

Key and acutely painful tooth socket containing base bone and broken down clot the patients complaints of continuous, severe throbbing pain that usually starts 3rd day after extraction management consists of irrigation of socket with warm saline followed by obtruding dressing.

Question - while extracting a mandibular third molar it is noted that the distal root is missing the root tip is most likely in the :-

a. Submental space
b. Pterygomandibular space
c. submandibular space
d. parapharyngeal space

Answer - c

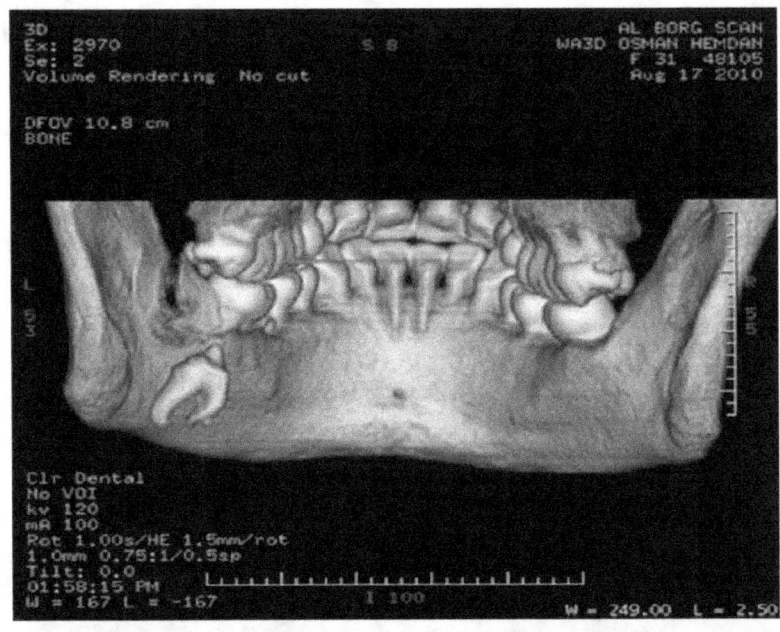

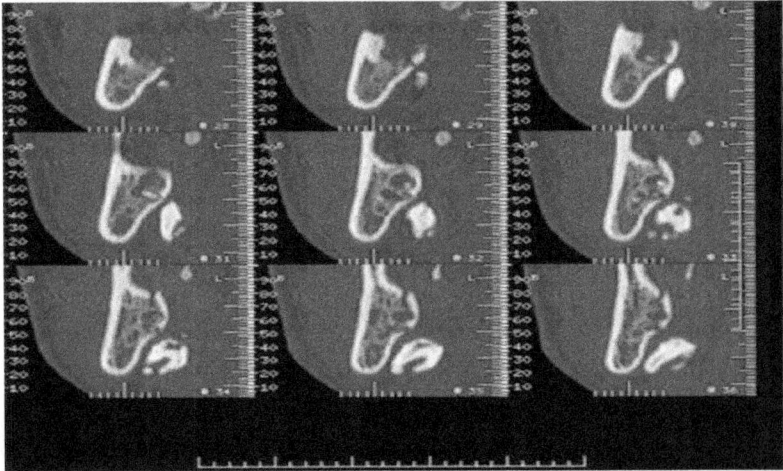

The location of root tip will depend on the position of 3rd molar if the tooth is vertically positioned the root tip is most likely in the submandibular space

If the tooth in mesioangular or horizontal position, it will be located in pterygomandibular space maxillary third molar is usually pushed into the infratemporal space.

Note: one day after complete month extraction blue black sports are seen on the neck of the patients theses sports indicate post operative ecchymosed (ecchymoses are large extravasations of blood into subcutaneous tissues with facial dislocation caused by breakdown of hemoglobin). The common area of past operative ecchymoses are circum orbital and submandibular regions lower lip and floor of mouth management consists of immediate application of cold followed by heat. In severe cases antibiotics are given along with proteolytic enzymes which causes breakdown of coagulated blood.

Facts:

The best time to administer analgesics is before anesthesia wears off

-extraction of a tooth during acute infection helps drainage and relieves pain if proper antibiotic is given and its adequate blood level is reached

-most important principle during extraction is least trauma to both bone and mucosa while extracting the tooth in pieces.

-diagnosis a dry socket is done by history.

-the principal action of ammonia in syncope is respiratory stimulant

- rubber band extraction is a method of extraction in patients having bleeding disorder like hemophilia and hemangioma

-hypoglycemia may occur in a patient taking insulin and undergoing extraction when extraction is done on empty stomach.

Question - radiographic appearance of the inferior dental canal and roots of mandibular third molar :-

    a. Tram lines visible

    b. Radiolucent band evident in relation to root of third molar which is grooved tunneled.

    c. Winter's lines

    d. Tram lines enhanced

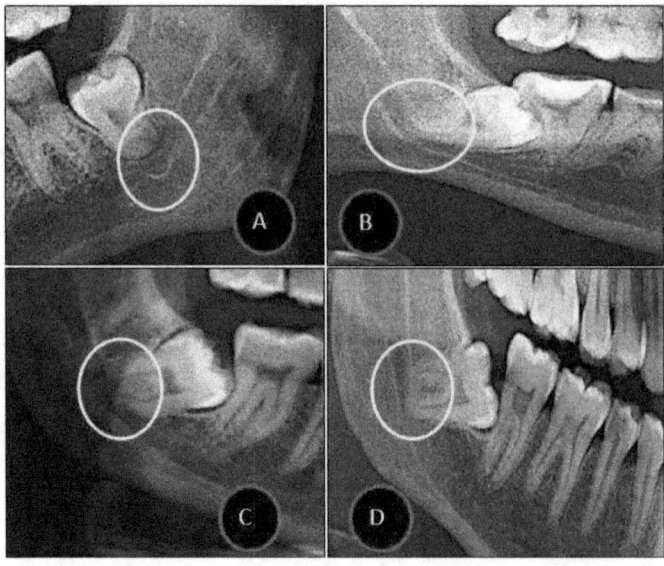

Radiographic Sign observed on digital OPG : A- Narrowing of canal, B – Diversion of canal, C – Darkening of root, D – Interruption of white line of canal.

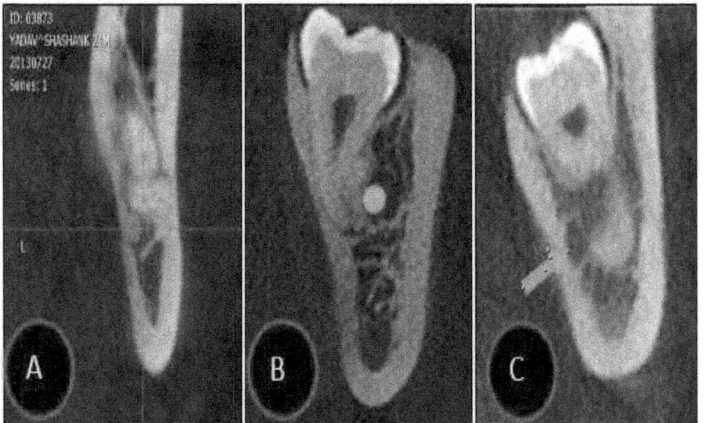

Cortical Plate Resorption Observed On CBCT : A – Buccal, B – Lingual, C – Intact.

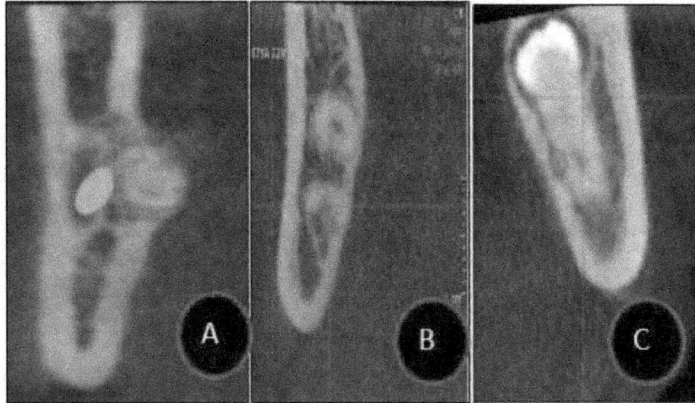

Position of inferior alveolar canal on CBCT : A – Buccal, B – Inferior / Interradicular, C – Lingual.

Question - extraction of disto angular impaction of mandibular 3rd molar can cause :-

a. Fracture of ramus
b. Slippage in lingual pouch
c. Excessive hemorrhage
d. Dry socket

Answer - a

Distoangular impaction is difficult to remove because of its pathway of delivery into ascending ramus. A large amount of bone removal is required which makes the ramus weak and more prone to fracture

Note: during extraction of lower impacted right molar bone is removed upto CEJ/ highest curvature of bulge of crown

The best treatment for pericoronitis involving an impacted mandibular third molar is extraction of the involved third molar

-distoangular impacted tooth is the most difficult impaction of a third molar

Question - in winter's WAR line, amber line represent ?

Answer - bone level covering the impacted tooth.

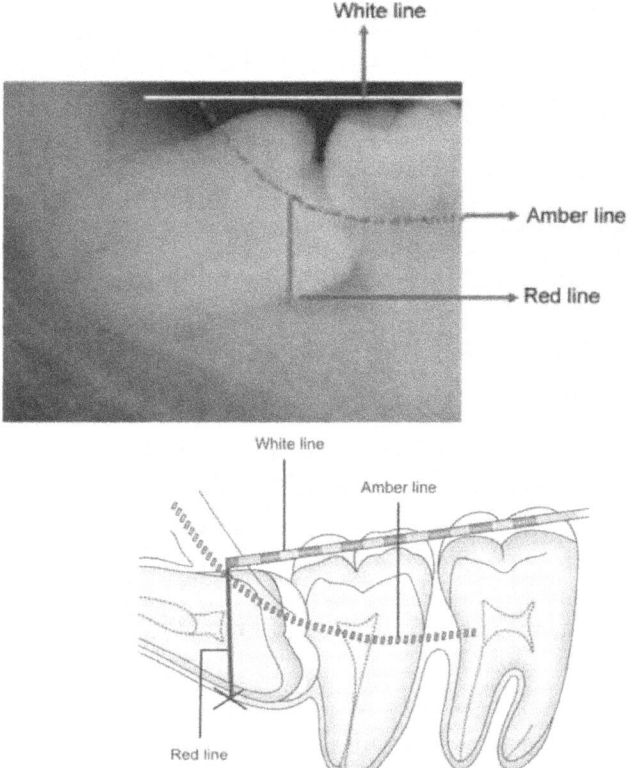

Tracing of WAR lines on a horizontally impacted mandibular third molar. White line is drawn along the occlusal surface of the erupted mandibular molars and extended posteriorly the third molar region. 'Amber' line is drawn from the surface of the bone lying distal to the third molar to the crest of the interdental septum between the first and second molar. 'Red' line is a perpendicular dropped from the 'amber' line to an imaginary 'point of application' of an elevator.

Question - after surgery of 3rd molar, patches of anesthesia on chin is due to damage of ?

Answer - inferior alveolar nerve

Question - after multiple tooth extraction, suture is placed at :-

a. Adjacent tooth
c. across the socket
b. Interdental septum
d. none of the above

Answer - b

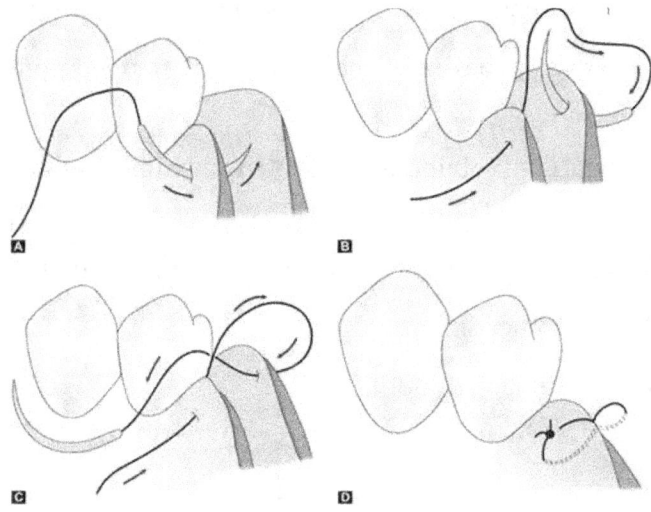

Question - mucoperiosteal flap ?

a. When raised do not cause postoperative swelling and pain
b. Are supinely raised during extraction
c. Are raised whenever bone removal is desisted to facilitate extraction
d. When raised will cause trauma and injury to underlying osseous tissues

Answer - d

Although the mucoperiosteal flaps are raised whenever bone removal is decided to facilitate extraction. But it is only one of the indication of mucoperiosteal flap elevation. But injury to the underlying periosteum and bone is invariably present even when the mucoperiosteal flap is raised without any bone removal

Question - the most common reason for the removal of impacted mandibular third molars ?

a. Orthodontic treatment
c. reffered pain
b. Chromic periodontal disease
d. recurrent pericoronitis

Answer - d

Question - the most common tooth to get impacted (excluding third molar) is ?

a. Mandibular canine
c. maxillary canine
b. Maxillary 2nd premolar
d. mandibular 2nd premolar

Answer - c

Question - post extraction bleeding in a leukaemic patient due to ?

a. Increase in leukocytes
b. Low calcium level
c. platelet disorder
d. deficiency of clothing factors

Answer - c

The sign and symptoms of acute leukemic result gross either bone narrow suppression or infiltration of leukemic cells into organ tissues. These changes cause anemia, thrombocytopenia and a decrease in neutrophils thrombocytopenic causes spontaneous bleeding such as petechiae ecchymoses epistaxis, it may necessary to perform surgery on patients with platelet counts in the range of 25000 because of the difficulty in achieving platelet levels due to circulating platelet antibodies.

Question - in wharfe assessment of impacted third molars "a stands for

a. Amber line
b. Axis of rotation
c. angulation of 3rd molar
d. application of elevator

Answer - c

The six factors chosen for scaring in wharfe assessment are:

-winters classification

-height of mandible

-angulations of third molar

-root shape

-follicle

-path of exit to tooth during removal.

When the inferior alveolar canal crosses the root apex, these is reduction in its diameter. This narrowing or converging appearance of the canal is due to displacement of the root and floor of the canal towards each other resulting is an "hourglass appearance this appearance indicates partial encirclement of the canal.

WHARFE'S ASSESSMENT		
Criteria	Category	Score
Winters Classifications	Horizontal	2
	Distoangular	2
	Mesioangular	1
	Vertical	0
Height of mandible	1-30 mm	0
	31-34 mm	1
	35-39 mm	2
Angulation of 3rd molar	1-50 deg.	0
	60-69	1
	70-79	2
	80-89	3
	90+	4

WHARFE'S ASSESSMENT		
Root shape & development	Complex	3 (more than 2/3 complete)
	unFavourable curvature	2 (less than 1/3 complete)
	favourable Curvature	1
Follicals	Normal	0
	Possibly enlarged	1
	Enlarged	2
Path of exit	Space available	0
	Distal cusps covered	1
	Mesial cusps also covered	2
	Both covered	3
TOTAL		33

Question - the difficulty score for mesioangular impacted mandibular 3rd molar class II & level II is ?

a. 5   c. 10
b. 7   d. 6

Answer - a

Difficulty index for removal of impacted lower third molars classification :

Angulation	difficulty index value
Mesioangular	1
Horizontal / tansverse	2
Vertical	3
Distoangular	4

Depth	
Level A	1
Level B	2
Level C	3

Ramus relationship / space available	
Class I	1
Class II	2
Class III	3

Very difficult	7 to 10
Moderate difficult	5 to 7
Minimally difficult	3 to 4

Question - A 55 year old patient of myocardial infection is on 75 mg aspirin for last 6 months. He has to undergo extraction of carious tooth, what the dentist should do ?

a. Extraction can be done as this dose of aspirin does not lead to marked bleeding during extraction.
b. Stop aspirin at least for 3 days prior to extraction
c. Stop aspirin at least for 7 days prior to extraction
d. Cannot perform extraction.

Answer - a

Anti platelet effect of aspirin is elected at low dose of 0.5 to 1.5 mg kg/day. Where analgesic and anti-inflammatory effects are achieved at dose of 5 to 10 mg/kg/day and more than 30mg/kg/day respectively. (note on solving the above does schedule for an average adult of 60 kg, the ant platelet does is 30 mg to 90 mg /kg/day

Conclusion: routine dental extraction can be safely done in patients on long term antiplatelet medication with no interruption do not have increased risk of prolonged or excessive postoperative bleeding.

Fact: the most posterior teeth are removed first

-when a tooth is lost there is decrease in trabecular pattern loss of bone with loss of bone height

-cardiac dysarrythmia during extraction is caused by trigeminal nerve

-lingual nerve is near to mandibular third molar (medial aspect) and is likely to be damaged while removing 3rd molar

-the ideal time for removal of impacted third molar is when the root of teeth are one – third formed and before they are two third formed.

Complications

Complications & Emergencies On Extraction Of Teeth

1. **Local Complication:-**
   a) Immediate
   b) Delayed
   c) Late

2. **Systemic Complication:-**
   d) Immediate
   e) Late

Local Complication:-

   a) Immediate
   1. Dislocation Of Adjacent Tooth
   2. Dislocation Of TMJ
   3. Failure To Remove Tooth
   4. Failure To Secure Anesthesia
   5. Damage To Gums, Lips, Inferior Alveolar Nerve Or Its Branches, Lingual Nerve, Tongue Floor Of The Mouth.
   6. Displacement Of Root Into Maxillary Antrum Soft Tissue.
   7. Hemorrhagic While Extraction Of Tooth On Completion Of Extraction.
   8. Fracture Of Crown, Root, Maxillary Tuberosity, Mandible, Opposite Tooth, Alveolar Bone.
   9. Swelling/Hematoma Formation.
   10. Oro-Antral Communication
   11. Burning On Injection
   12. Broken Needles

   b) Delayed
   1. Prolonged Anesthesia Or Paresthesia.
   2. Open Wound/ Unhealed Wound.
   3. Aggressive Pain.
   4. Swelling.
   5. Trismus.

6. Hemorrhage.
7. Dry Socket.
8. Infection.
9. Oro-Antral Fistula.
10. Traumatic Arthritis To TMJ.
11. Osteomyelitis.

c) Late
1. Chronic Oesteomylitis.
2. Chronic Pain.
3. Nerve Damage.
4. Osteoradionecrosis.
5. Sloughing Of Tissues.
6. Postanesthetic Intraoral Lesions.

Systemic (Immediate)
1. Syncope
2. Respiratory Arrest.
3. Cardiac Arrest/Myocardial Infarction.
4. Hypoglycemia
5. Shock
6. Respiratory Obstruction
7. Adrenal Crisis.
8. Hyperventilation Syndrome.
9. Epileptic Seizures.
10. Allergic Reactions.
11. Pregnancy(Supine Hypotensive Syndrome).

LATE
1. Aids
2. Sepsis

Medical Emergencies:-

Related To Cardiovascular
a) Angina pectoris
b) Coronary artery disease.

- c) Shock.
- d) Hypertension.
- e) Congestive heart failure.
- f) Hpotension.
- g) Cardiac arrhythmias.

Related To Blood

- a) Leukemia
- b) Haemophilia.
- c) Thrombocytopenic purpura.

Related To Metabolic Diseases

- a) Diabetes.
- b) Cholinesterase inactivity.

Related To CNS

- a) Epilepsy.
- b) Syncope.
- c) Cerebral vascular accidents.

Related To Respiration

- a) Emphysema.
- b) Mechanical respiratory embarrassment.
- c) Asthma.

Related To Endocrine

- a) Hypothyroidism.
- b) Hyperthyroidism.
- c) Adrenal insufficiency.

Related To Prescribed Drugs

Dislocation of adjacent teeth:-

- Use the elevator properly.
- Use proper finger support/stabilization to the adjacent teeth.
- Do not apply the elevator on mesial aspect of first molar, it may lead to displacement/ subluxation of adjacent second premolar.

- Grasp elevator tightly so that the instrument cannot slip from their intended site of action to damage the adjacent teeth.
- Direct force may apply to the adjacent tooth if the adjacent tooth is to be removed at the same visit or else force should be transmitted via interseptal bone to the adjacent tooth to prevent from subluxation or damage.

Dislocation of TMJ:-

Operator should wrap a gauze in both the thumb finger and place the thumb in lower posterior teeth (posterior most) the remaining four fingers under the lower border of mandible. push down the molar teeth by rotating the chin upward in the glenoid fossa.

- If resistance or pain encounters the patient proceede with the same procedure under local anesthesia.(same as PSA block).
- In completely or partially edentulous patient the operator stand in front of the patient & place the thumb inta-orally on the external oblique ridges and apply the downward & upward movement of mandible simultaneously warned the patient not to yawn too widely, not to open the mouth for a few days post reduction of jaw & an extra oral support to the jaw / joint should be applied. Do the baryl bandage.

Failure to remove the tooth:-

The reason behind this is most likely

a) Either the bone texture is dense & inelastic.

b) The root shape is obstructing its path of withdrawl.

If fails to remove non surgically, then go with the surgical procedure by reflection of mucoperiosteal flap & remove the bone with the help of chisel mallete or micromotor hand piece or divide the tooth / root asindicated.

Failure to secure anesthesia:-

- The first most common error to secure anesthesia is the inaccurate placement of injection needle to the anatomic site.
- Second most common error is injection of too small dose & third most important error is not waiting long enough for the anesthesia to act.
- Before going for extraction, check the tooth with a blunt probe by moving around the crevice or around the gingiva, or by taping the tooth with a instrument. If no. pain, get the extraction done.
- In case the tooth is involved by periodontitis, intra ligamental, intra osseous or intrapulpal injection may be indicated.
- Do not inject the local anesthetic solution to the infected tissue, it may lead to spread the infection.
- Explain the patient that, he / she may feel pressure on extraction.

Damage to the soft tissue:-

The most common cause is not handling in a correct way to the elevator. Elevators should always be held with the index finger down the shank of the handle towards the tip to act as a 'stop' in case the instrument slips.

- While using scalpel and periosteal elevator or scissors operator should have a good command on his / her hand so that it should not slip off.
- The lower lip get easily trapped in between the handles of forcep while applying force to the tooth. So better to retract the lip with the fingers of the opposite hand.

Before attempting extraction of the lower molar, always get an IOPA or OPG done, so that one can rule out the relationship of Inferior alveolar nerve to the root

Do not attempt to remove the lower broken root piece if the inferior alveolar nerve is in very close contact to the root instrument may get into the nerve and can damage it.

Directly do not grasp the gingiva while extraction, first reflect the, attachment interdental papilla well.

Always use the retractor while using cutting bur in the extraction of lower molar and use the lower molar forcep carefully so that lingual soft tissue did not get trapped in the beak of forcep ,it may damage the lingual nerve along with lingual soft tissue.

Care should be taken when using chisel mallet on lingual split technique it may damage the lingual nerve.

At the time of discharge, place a cotton roll between the lips and teeth which is secured by dental floss or suture.

NOTE : Securing the cotton roll is important because the patient did not get swallow accidently because of the numbness of lips and tongue.

If any of these happens, prescribe antibiotics and analgesics along to the vitamin B complex and tell the patient to go lukewarm saline rinses.

Displacement Of Root Into Maxillary Antrum :-

- Improper application of forceps to a tooth or elevating a root inadequate access may cause such displacement.
- Do not apply forceps to a root below the antrum until the operator can not grasp the root sufficiently under direct vision.
- By chance if the root get break from the apical third, specially palatal roots of maxillary molar, do not try to attempt for removal of apical piece of root (if the length is less than 5mm).
- Nerve attempt to retrieve a root below the antrum by passing an instrument up into the socket. Instead of doing this procedure go to the lateral approach technique by raising the buccal flap and removing the bone by tapping or rotary
- In case if it encounter go to sinus exploration and root retrieval.

- If a tooth or root is lost from the view during the course of an extraction rule out clinically and radiographically to the patient it may enter into the following sites :-
    a) Into the stomach
    b) Into the lung
    c) Into the antrum
    d) Into the soft tissue space
    e) Into the suction apparatus
    f) Get a chest x-ray done and OPG done

Haemorrhage :-
- Operator should know the blood report or any history of previous bleeding during tooth extraction (Hemophilic or platelet deficiency patient are more likely of bleeding disorder.
- Place a gauze pack over the socket for 10 min by applying billing force and instruct not to disturbthe clot by any activity like chewing, rinsing, check the figure or tongue etc.
- Use high vaccume suction ,use vasoconstrictor
- Use oxidised cellulose gauze (surgical –ethicon) and horizontal mattresses suture
- Use bone wax if the bleeding is from cancellous bone
- Put the extracted tooth again in the extraction socket to prevent from bleeding
- If all else fails then packing the socket gauze soaked in whitehead varnish (compound idoform paint) is a reliable to the problem but the pack must be removed after 10 days.
- Check the systemic issues of the patient whether he/she is on anticoagulant ,aspirin ,NSAID.
- If blood loss is more than 30% it may require blood transfusion.

Precaution :-
a) Stop aspirin 1week before extraction
b) Oozing can be stop by applying hot salin pack for 2 min.
    - Oozing can be stop by swabbing by gauze pack or by use of sucker (pressure20 Ib/sg in)
    - On secondary haemorrhage instruct the patient to place a large sponge given cloth ,or handkerchief (never absorbent cotton) tea bag (tannic acid acts as a stringent) over the haemorrhaging site, close firmly.
    - Use bone wax in crushed bone.
    - If from soft tissue, use Local anesthetic vasoconstrictor injection. Clamping, tying, electro coagulation, cryotherapy, monsel solution pack (ferric subsulfate – Astringent), suture may be placed over bleeding tissue. Simple nemonics ; 3P's and 5S 's

    Pressure, posture, patience

    Sedative, saline pack, styptic, suture, splint.

Fracture of the crown, root, maxillary tuberosity, mandible, opposite tooth, alveolar bone : -

- This occur by one of the following region -
a) Haste due to impatience or frustration
b) Unfavourable root anatomy
c) When excessive force is applied to a tooth
d) If the root /tooth is weaken by carries usrestoral
e) Improper extraction technique
f) Wrong forcep selection / or elevator selection
- In few situation the root fragment should be left untouched.

Example : If the apical 1/3rd root of max. molar broke down better to leave the root in its place because attempting to remove the root piece may get complicated if it get pushed into maxillary antrum or in case of mandibular molar it may go into inferior alveolar nerve.

Note : Thumb rule is if the apical root piece is 5mm or less than 5mm better to leave in its position until not indicated very strongly

- For a short period, place a cotton wool in corporated zinc oxide and eugenol cloves oil into the fractured fragment.

Fractured of Alveolar Bone : -

- Labial plate get easily fractured on extraction of canine teeth
- Alveolar bone may get weaken by the involved pathology or unfavovurable Alveolar anatomy

Note : Alveolar bone has been weakened by extraction of the lateral incisor or 1st premolar prior to the removal of cave. If these three teeth are to be extracted at one visit the incidence of the labial plate will be reduced if the canine is removed first.

- Remove the alveolar fragment which has lost over on half of its periosteal attachment.

Fracture of adjacent tooth : -

- In case of bridge / multiple crown is placed better to devide a vulcarbo or diamond disk before extraction if the tooth is abutment tooth
- Remove the overhanged restoration from the adjacent teeth
- Do not use the adjacent tooth as a full crown until the adjacent tooth also to be extracted at same visit

Fracture of maxillary tuberosity :-

- If this encounter raise the large buccal mucoperiosteal flap and closed the fractured site mattress suture and left the suture for 10 days.

Fracture of the mandible :-
- Rule out the following abnormalities clinically, Radiographically and histopathologically if suspected Tumors, cyst, Hyperparathyroidism, fibrous dysplasia, osteoporosis, atropy, osteomyelitis osteodystrophis, therapeutic irridation, unerupted teeth. Inform the patient about the complication if get fractured do the surgical procedure like – ORIF or non surgical procedure like MMF.

Swelling / Hematoma formation : -
- Apply direct pressure at the site of bleeding at least 2 min.
- Apply pressure on the medial aspect of the ramus of mandible if the cause is inferior alveolar nerve block
- ASA nerve block, Pressure is placed directly over the infra orbital foramen
- Buccal nerve block or palatal nerve block the clinical manifestation of hematoma seen intraorbital so direct pressure is applied at the bledding site intraorally
- Metal or incisive nerve block pressure is directly placed either intra orally or extraorally on the mental foramen region
- PSA Nerve block digital pressure should apply intra orally medially and superiorly direction andplace the ice pack extraorally anterior to the auricule
- If soreness develops, advise the patient to take aspirin or NSAID
- Do not apply heat to the area for 4-6 hour initially
- Heat may be applied to the next day 20 min /hour.
- Patient will recover after 1- 2 week, till then no dental treatment continue.

Oro-antral Communication and fistula :

Symptom of mnemonics 4E's Symtopms of fistula 5P's

- Escape of fluid - Pain
- Escape of air - phonation problem
- Enhanced air column - persistent purulent
- Epistaxis (not always) postnasal drip
- poppin of antral pathology orally

Tests to perform for oral – antral communication :-
1) Place a cotton wisf infront of nasal opening and ask the patient to exhale through nose closed mouth. In case of communication, wisp will move because of air passing from nose through the hole into oral cavity.
2) Ask the patient to fill the mouth colored water and let him / her bend downward and forward the colored water will flow out from the nose if the communication is there.

Oro – antral fistula

- Recently extend communication   - Established OAF
  |
  Don't explore sharp instrument.
  |
      Primary closure   -Buccal flap : Reharmann flap
      |
      Acrylic splint   : Moczair flap
                                        : Buccal fat pad
                                        -Palatal flap
                                        - Combination flap

NOTE : Sucker tips or probes should not be pushed up into the antrum as this manure could creat a communication.

Prescribe the medication : Antibiotic, Anti inflammatory, Anti allergic, Nasal decongestant, steam inhalation.

Burning on injection :

- Do not exceed the recommended rate of injection i.e, 1.8 ml /min. The ideal rate of infusion is 1 m /min
- The anesthetic cartilage should be stored at room temp. in the container (blister – pack or tin) or in alcohol free container.

Broken needles :-

- Do not inject the needle surprisingly to the patient rather inform the patient before insertion of needle

Note : Thumb rule is leave the needle out in view atleast 1/3rd. Do not insert the full length of the needle.

- Do not use resterilizable needle – needle becomes dull
- Do not use a needle too fine i.e. 27 ,30 gauze needle in the deeper tissue. this is used for superficial injection.
- Do not change the direction of inserted needle when it is stuck in bone
- Do not attempt to force a needle against resistance.
- Once the needle is broke down try to retrieve the broken needle with the help of sharp beak instrument.

Delayed

Prolonged anesthesia and paraesthesia:-

- Patient returned to normal without treatment but duration is not specific. It may take few hours, few days, 3 month, 6 month, 12 month or even more than 12 month sometimes (defend on the level of damage).

Note:- The damage from the needle itself result in hyperalgesia & not anesthesia.

- Mild Symptoms:- anti-inflammatory medication moderate example:- Ibuprofen or aspirin.
- Severe paresthesia – antidepressant, example- amitriptyline.
- Severe paresthesia - opium derivatives, example-

codeine Prescribe- multivitamins.

Delayed wound healing :- If the patient is diabetic or having high B.P, control the disease first maintain good oral hygiene.

- Analgesics & antibiotics.
- Irrigation with warm saline to remove debris.
- Chlorhexidine mouth wash
- Extending the denture to cover the extraction sockets.
- Place the suture in the extraction socket secondary if required.
- Check for the presence of an infected retained root or a piece of dead bone (sequestrum). The socket may be found to be full of malignant tumour.
- Persisting infections of bone (osteomyelitis) & oro- antral fistulae may also be the cause of problem.

Aggressive pain :-

- Rule out the underlying cause.
- Suitable analgesic medication prescribe the patient & the route of drug administration should be IV. Eg- NSAIDs, acetaminophen, Cox-2 inhibitors, antidepressants & anti-seizure medications & opoids.

Edema / Swelling :-

- Do not inject the solution traumatic.
- Do not inject the irritating solution.
- If swelling is because of infection, prescribe antibiotic therapy.
- If the cause is allergy, prescribe Intra muscular or oral histamine beta blocker.
- Using blunt instrument, traumatic flap design, use of rotary instrument into the soft tissue may lead to this problem so better to avoid such things in dental practice.

- Do not tie the suture too tightly it may cause sloughing of the soft tissues & breakdown of the suture line. Once swelling starts.
- Advice leukwarm water rinse & cold pack application extra-orally.

Trismus:-

Trismus may occur because of irritating solution. Haemorrhage, infection, edema. The dentist must merelyascertain the cause & prescribe the medication.

- Prevented by using sharp & sterile needles.
- Avoid reinjection the syringe in the same area.
- If the cause is trauma – advice exercises and muscle relaxants eg:-diazepam 2.5 to 5.0 mg (QID)or meprobamate 1200 to 1600 mg/day in 5-4 doses.
- Warm heat application-20 minutes/hr.
- Advice opening & closing of mouth exercise 10-15 min / 3-4 hr & lateral movement 10-15 min/3-4 hr.
- If the cause is infection – advice suitable antibiotic depending on severity.

Dry Socket:-

- Gentle irrigation of the socket to remove debris & loose bone particles should be carried induce the fresh bleeding out using warm saline & a sedative dressing on a small piece of ribbon gauze inserted into the opening of the wound. Patient need to be seen several times & dressing renewed every few days to maintain pain relief.
- With the help of bone rongeur & bone files, smoothen al the sharp bony ridge's & spicules.

Note:- While ZOE dressing relieve pain they also delay healing.

- A small pompom or ribbon guaze is left inside the dry socket for 2,3 weeks & the socket will fill up with the granulation tissues.

Note:- Inserting Pom-Pom is less painful than placing a ribbon – guaze pack.

- White head's varnish can also be prescribed for this.

Composition of White head varnish is –

Benzoin, Sumatra in coarse powder (3g)

Prepared Storax (2g)

Balsam of Tolu (1.5g)

Iodoform (3g) Solvent

ether 28.4 ml

Advice medications – antibiotics & anti anaerobic agent like metronidazole, analgesics & anti-inflammatory drugs.

Infection:-
- If the infection is by pyogenic bacteria. It may lead to collection large pus. This must be trainedas a priorities in the treatment.
- If the swelling is fluctuant in the buccal sulcus, it should be drained with an incision made through the mucosa.
- Sometimes extra- oral approach may required for incision & drainage. eg – ludwig's angina.

Oro-Antral Fistula

Conservative Treatment:-
- Daily antral lavage through the socket.
- Enlarge the socket if need for irrigation with warm saline using a bulb syringe.

Permanent closure can be done once the infection is subside.

Surgical Approach:-
- Buccal mucoperiosteal flap
- Palatal mucoperiosteal flap
- Palatal island flap
- Bridge flap
- Gold foil technique.

Traumatic Arthritis Of The TMJ:-
- Use the non- operated hand below the angle of mandible while extracting the teeth.
- If the operator knows the patient has a history of chronic dislocation of TMJ, it is adviced to get him hold a dental prop tightly between his/her teeth on the contralateral side during a dental extraction.

Osteomyelitis:-

Acute osteomyelitis requires high dose of an appropriate antibiotic for an extended period late chronic suppurative osteomyelitis requires surgical debridement of the affected area to remove any sequestra of dead bone.

Osteoradionecrosis:-

Conservtive Management:-

HBOT (hyperbaric oxygen therapy. Stage I or early stage of ORN is managed conservatively with therapies such as wound care, HBOT, antibiotic medications. Stage III advanced stage ORN is mnaged surgically with wide resection & immediate microvascular reconstruction for stage II or intermediate stage ORN, it is difficult to recommend a definitive treatment procedure.

Antibiotic usually penicillin with metronidazole or clindamycin is initially administered until bacterial identification is available.

Surgical Management:- including wound debridement which involves the removal of infected & devitalized teeth & associated soft tissue, sequestrectomy, which is the removal of devitlized bony fragments or an involucrum of the jaw, decortication, which is the removal of lateral & inferior cortical plates of bones to gain access to the infected medullary cavity & resection with healthy bony margins with immediate or delayed reconstruction.

Recent Treatment Approach

Pentoxifylline, Tocopherol, combination of both ,Clodronate, or combination of all three.

Sloughing of tissues:-

- If there is no epithelial desquamation or if there is sterile abscess, no formal management is necessary.
- For pain related factor prescribe the analgesics like aspirin or any NSAID'S.
- Prescribe oral ointment like orabase / Hexedine gel.

Post anesthetic inta-oral lesion :-

- Do not prescribe any analgesic medicine until the pain the severe.
- For ulceration prescribe the topical anesthetic gel solution.
- Advice mouth rinsing diphenhydramine & milk of analgesia for oral ulceration.
- Never advice corticosteroid.

Note:- Corticosteroid is not prescribed because of its anti-inflammatory actions exaggerate the risk of viral or bacterial accumulation.

Systemic Complication:-

1. **Overdose**

   - Mild overdose.

- Maintain the position first if the ptient is unconscious make the supine positon with elevated feet. If the patient is conscious maintain the position as the patient is comfortable with maintaining the airway, maintain the breathing, maintain the blood & fluid circulation (if needed give CPR) & manage the definitive care.

Under definitive care:-

- Administer O_2 via nasal cannula / nasal blood.
- Maintain the vital signs like Blood Pressure, Respiratory rate, temperature.
- Administer midazolam at the rate of 1mg/min if required.
- Discontinue the further dental treatment till the patient do not recover well.

- Severe overdose:-
- Maintain the position of the patient airway, breathing and circulation.

Under definitive care:-
- Administer anticonvulsant. If the seizure is prolonged for 4-5 min via parentral drug administration route.
- First line of drug is midazolam via IV at the rate of 1mg/min until seizures cease. If IV do not found then administer midazolam via IM or IV at the rate of 5mg/ml at the dose of 0.2mg/kg for adult to pediatric patient.

Note:-IV midazolam can prescribe less then 50kg at the dose of 0.2 mg kg up to 10mg.

2. Syncope:-

Lie down in supine position/lower the back of chair

↓

Raise the leg

Note:- The head of the patient should be at a lower level than the feet (to improve the venous return to the heart & oxygenated blood to the brain)

↓

Loosen the tight clothing

↓

Touch the cold sponges to the face or ask the patient to inhale the aromatic spirit of amonia

↓

If cyanosis is developing administer 100% O_2

↓

Record the vital signs

↓

If bradycardia inject atropine 0.6 mg diluted in 5ml of sterile H_2O IV

↓

If hypotension persists vasopressor drugs like phenylephrine or methxamine should be administered

↓

If unconsciousness persists for more than 5-10 min causes other than vasovagal syncope should be considered

↓

3. **Respiratory arrest:-**

$$\text{Laid down the patient on the floor}$$
$$\downarrow$$
$$\text{Clear the airway by removing any appliance or foreign bodies}$$
$$\downarrow$$
$$\text{Compress the patients nostrils with the fingures}$$
$$\downarrow$$
$$\text{Perform mouth – to – mouth rescuscitation}$$
$$\downarrow$$
$$\text{Check the carotid pulse \& apex beat at regular interval}$$
$$\downarrow$$
$$\text{If pulse \& apex beat cannot be felt \& heart sound cannot be heard than proceed with CPR}$$

4. **Cardiac arrest :-**

$$\text{Start the CPR}$$
$$\downarrow$$
$$\text{Maintain the O}_2 \text{ \& vital signs}$$
$$\downarrow$$
$$\text{Do this until an antomated exerted defibrillation (AED) becomes available}$$
$$\downarrow$$
$$\text{Provide Beta blockers/ACE inhibitors \& calcium channel blockers}$$
$$\downarrow$$
$$\text{Bleeding vessels should be ligated, stop the blood by crushing the bone or appliying pressure pack}$$
$$\downarrow$$
Restore the cost body fluids, blood should be replaced with blood, if in case the blood is not availalable the infuse with plasma expander or ringer's lactate solution. In the mean time arrange the blood
$$\downarrow$$
In case if RBC are not lost then plasma or plasma volume expanders are used as substitute. If haemoglobin is fallen down due to anaemia but there is no blood loss packed cells are given
$$\downarrow$$
Administer 100% oxygen
$$\downarrow$$
Assess the vital signs (BP, RR, PR)
$$\downarrow$$

Inject hydrocortisone sodium hemisuccinate 100 mg dissolved in 5ml of sterile water is given IV. In case of adrenal insufficiency larger dose may required.

↓

In case of hypotension inject mephentermine

↓

If pulse is weak inject atrophine IV 0.6 mg diluted water till the radial pulse becomes palpable

↓

Prescribe IV route antibiotics

Hypoglycemia:- The rule of 15 for treating hypoglycaemia if blood glucose is < 70 mg/dl.

1. Consume 15 gm of carbohydrate.
2. After 15 mins check blood glucose.
3. If blood glucose is still<70 m/dl, consume another 15 gm of carbohydrate.
4. Repeat step 2& 3 until blood glucose increases to 70 mg/dl.
5. Once blood glucose is normalized, consume a snack or meal containing complex carbohydrates & protein in order to avoid recurrence of hypoglycemia.

If the patient is not able to eat:-

Administer 20ml of 50% dextrose IV bolus and then 5 or 10% dextrose fluids IV at 100 ml/h until stabilized. If available injection 1mg (1ml) single dose can be administered instead of dextrose.

Shock:-

The step by step treatment of shock should be aimed at preventing and treating hypoxia of vital organs.

- Put the patient in such a position that the head at lower level than the feet (15^0 trendelenburg position)

↓

Maintain the body heat by keeping a hot water bottle inside touching the patient body surface & covering the patient with a blanket over.

↓

Maintain the airway of the patient

↓

In neurogenic anaphylactic & septicemic shock, inject adrenaline (to rise the BP of patient one ampule of 1:1000 dilution is further diluted in 10ml of sterile H_2O, 0.5 ml of this solution is given IV slowly, one drop / min till a good thrust is felt for the radial pulse.

↓

Prescribe narcotic analgesic for pain relief

(**Note**:- do not recommend narcotic is respiratory distress & head injury)

↓

Respiratory obstruction by foreign body :-

It can be assisted by leaving the patient at the back & neck. Small children can be held upside down from the legs & gentle blows over the back are given.

↓

If not helpful lie down the patient in the dental chair or the floor, tilt the head of the patient to one side, push down the index & middle finger in the deep throat to grasp any material or instrument.

↓

Dislodge the object to expelled by forceful cough

↓

If not helpful, perform the Heimlich procedure by sitting or standing patient is grasped from the waist area by standing at his back & forceful upward thrust is exerted. Alternatively in a lying down patient pressure is applied on the abdomen is an upward directions at a level above the naval & below the ribcage.

↓

If pushed down to larynx arrange the laryngoscope & magill forceps for removal of foregin body.

↓

May required tracheotomy or tracheostomy in emergency

Adrenal crisis:-

Stop the further dental treatment

↓

Put the patient in shock position

↓

Maintain the airway & administer

↓

Start IV line with 5% dextrose saline

↓

Administer 100-200 mg hydrocortisone sodium succinate IV

↓

The dose may be repeated if no response is seen

Hyperventilation Syndrome :-

Instructing the patient to breath slowly & deeply into a paper bag at the rate of 10 times / min.

↓

Ask the patient to hold the breath for sometime to reverse the respiratory alkalosis.

↓

In emergency close the mouth & nostrils by placing a hand to bring the respiration rate down.

Seizure:-

Maintain the airway

↓

Prevent anybodily injury from occurring the convulsion

↓

IV pentobarbital sodium (Nembertal) or secobarbital sodium (sectional) given.

↓

Ventilate with or may be given 20-40 mg of succinylcholine chloride IV or double the dose IM.

Allergic reactions :-

a. Antihistaminic agents (Benadryl, 20 to 50 mg).

b. Isoproterenol or epinephrine inhalation.

c. Epinephrine (0.5 ml of 1:1000 intramuscularly).

d. Aminophylline (0.5 mg IV).

e. Oxygen.

Pregnancy:-(Supine hypotension syndrome)

- Avoid all surgical procedure during the first trimester to avoid premature labour.
- Patient must be relieved of stress & strain and painful experiences.
- A patient developing supine hypotension syndrome should be turned to left side in the reclining posture and constantly reassured for a quick recovery.

Medical Conditions:-

CVS

1. Hypotension / Hypertension / Cardiac arrhythmias:-

    Patient treated for the symptoms with O_2 positioning & administration of narcotic analgesics.

CHF:- Note:- if patient becomes anxious, discontinue all the dental procedure, a moist cough sometimes producing a pink- tinged sputum. Maintain the semi sitting position of the patient. Provide O_2, medicines prescribed through IM route – Morphine 8-10 mg or meperidine 50 to 7 mg.

Angina Pectoris:-

Tablet of nitroglycerine 0.6 mg should be given sublingually or asked the patient to inhale amyl nitite. if do not recover, administer O_2, IM / IV – meperidine or morphine to get relief with pain and anxiety.

Coronary artery occlusion:-

Administer O_2
↓
Maintain the supine position of the patient with the head & thorax elevated
↓
IM / IV – morphine (8-15mg/ meperidine (50-100 mg)

Emphysema:-

Bronchodilator sprays containing 1:1000 epinephrine or 1:200 isoproterenol should be prescribed.

Nervous System Disorder:-

Cerebral vascular accidents:-

Maintain the oxygen level of the patient with the help of ventilation.
↓
Consult physician

Metabolic Disease:-

Diabetic coma:-

No treatment will be given from the dentist side.

Insulin shock :-

Provide lumps of sugar / sweets or sweet drinks
↓
IM / IV glucagon hydrochloride (0.5-1 mg)
↓
IV dextrose 5% or 10 % in H_2O.

Cholinesterase inactivity:-

Endocrine malfunction :- Hypothyroidism

- Lower done the dose of prescribed medicine.
- Regular respiration & circulation if needed.
- Prescribe narcotic antagonist (naloxone).
- Emergencies from prescribed medication.

Respiratory

Asthma:-

Mild attack – Requires no specific treatment.

Severe — Administer oxygen
↓

(**Note**:- Administer the O_2 accordingly, it may cause air tapping because inspiration is much less effected than expiration).
↓

IM epinephrine 0.3 to 0.5 ml of 1:1000 solution.

Or

IV aminophylline 0.25 to 0.5mg
↓
Bronchodilator spray that contains isotrenol in 1:200 solution.
↓
If not recovered, repeat this for 10- 20min.

Mechanical respiratory embarrassment:-

If the foreign object is stucked in pharynx.
↓
Ask the patient to open the mouth
↓
Ask not to take deep inhalation breathing & not to swallow.
↓
Using Kelly forceps try If fails, to retrieve the object
↓
If fails, ask the patient to cough forcefully.

Note:- If the object get stucked in the glottis, it may cause partial laryngospasm
↓
If required, perform cricothyrotomy.

Hyperthyroidism:-

- Prescribe the sedative drugs.
- Apply the cold pack to the patient to lower down the body temperature.
- Supply O_2.

Adrenal insufficiency:-

5% dextrose in H_2O or CR solution IV.
↓
Maintain the BP
↓
Give hydrocortisone succinate 100-200mg / dexamethasone 4-12 mg IV.
↓
If BP do not return to normal phenylephrine / mephentarmine sulphate IV
↓
Provide O_2 support to the patient.

Bibliography

1) Handbook of local anesthesia, seventh edition, Stanley F. Malamed, ISBN: 9780323582070.

2) The extraction of teeth, Geoffrey L. Howe, Second edition, ISBN 0-72362231-0.

3) Monheim's Local Anesthesia & Pain Control in dental practice, C. Richard Bennett, Seventh edition.

4) Local anesthesia manual, Loma Linda University School Of Dentistry, Barry Krall.

5) Tooth Extraction , A Practical Guide, Paul D. Robinson,Jsb40-7256-1071-1.

6) Exodontia Practice, Abhay N Datarkar.

7) Text Book Of Oral And Maxillofacial Surgery – 3rd Edition, Prof Dr. Neelima Anil Malik, Isbn 9789350259382.

8) Dental Pulse, 15th Edition, K. Satheesh Kumar Reddy, Isbn – 10: 8194699053.

9) Aiims-25, Postgraduate Dental Entrance Examination, 2nd Edition , Aman Sharma , Sandeep Goyal, Simranjit Singh, Isbn- 9789386310354.

10) All India Postgraduate Dental Entrance Exam , 10th Edition, Neeraj Wadhwan, Isbn-13: 978-8195498147.

11) Dentest Clinical Sciences, Sgowri Shankar, Suresh Shenvi, Isbn-10: 818914996

12) Neet Mds Medical Entrance Exam, Isbn- 13: 978-9390893713, Isbn – 10: 9390893712.

13) Target Mds Neet, Mohit Gautam, Gaurav Anand, Isbn -10: 938191057.

14) Dental Triplet, Aman Sharma, Simranjit Singh, Sandeep Goyal, Isbn – 13:978-9390758562, Isbn – 10 : 9390758564.

15) Brahmastra For Pgi Dental Mds Entrance Exams, Varun Chopra, Radhika Chopra, Pankaj, Isbn – 13:978-8184452198.

16) Dental Companion Series Oral Suurgery, Dams Publications, Isbn-93-87503-73-9.

17) Mcqs In Clinical Dentistry 2021, 1st Edition, Dr. Ashokan Ck, Isbn-13:978-1639404681, Isbn-10:1639404686.

18) Mossby's Review For The Nbde, 2nd Edition, Isbn-978-81-312-3886-8.

19) Dento- Gulf, A Complete Book For Gulf Countries Dentistry Licence Exams- 3rd Edition, Mahalingham K, Isbn-10:9386480824, Isbn- 13: 978-9386480828.

20) Manual Of Local Anesthesia In Dentistry – 3rd Edition, Ap Chitra, Isbn -13: 978-9352501984, Isbn-10: 9352501985.

21) Local Anesthetics: Review Of Pharmacological Considerations, Daniel E. Becker, and Kenneth L. Reed, Anesth Prog 59:90^102 2012, Received January 10, 2012; accepted for publication February 20, 2012, ISSN 0003-3006/12.

22) Berde CB, Strichartz GR. Local anesthetics. In: Miller RD, Eriksson LI, Fleisher LA, et al, eds. Miller's Anesthesia. 7th ed. Philadelphia, Pa: Elsevier, Churchill Livingstone; 2009.

23) Katzung BG, White PF. Local anesthetics. In: Katzung BG, Masters SB, Trevor AJ, ed. Basic and Clinical Pharmacology. 11th ed. New York, NY: McGraw-Hill Companies Inc; 2009.

24) Goodson JM, Moore PA. Life-threatening reactions after pedodontic sedation: an assessment of narcotic, local anesthetic and antiemetic drug interactions. J Am Dent Assoc. 1983;107:239^245.

25) Schatz M. Adverse reactions to local anesthetics. Immunol Allergy Clin North Am. 1992;12:585^609.

26) Gell PGH, Coombs RRA. Classification of allergic reactions responsible for clinical hypersensitivity and disease. In: Gell PGH, Coombs RRA, Hachmann PJ, ed. Clinical Aspects of Immunology. 3rd ed. Oxford, England: Blackwell Scientific; 1975.

27) Adkinson NF Jr. Drug allergy. In: Adkinson NF Jr, Yunginger JW, Busse WW, et al, eds. Middleton's Allergy: Principles and Practice. 6th ed. Philadelphia, Pa: Mosby Inc; 2003.

28) Gall H, Kaufmann R, Kalveram CM. Adverse reactions to local anesthetics: analysis of 197 cases. J Allergy Clin Immunol. 1996;97:933^937.

29) Montamat SC, Cusack BJ, Vestal RE. Management of drug therapy in the elderly. N Engl J Med. 1989;321: 303^309.

30) Raymond SA, Gissen AJ. Mechanisms of differential block. In: Strichartz GR, ed. Local Anesthetics. Berlin, Germany: Springer, 1987:95–164.

31) Kunze H, Nahas N, Traynor JR, Wurl M. Effects of local anaesthetics on phospholipases. Biochim Biophys Acta. 1976;441:93–102.

32) Ring J, Franz R, Brockow K. Anaphylactic reactions to local anesthetics. Chem Immunol Allergy. 2010;95:190–200.

33) Batinac T, Sotošek Tokmadžić V, Peharda V, Brajac I. Adverse reactions and alleged allergy to local anesthetics: analysis of 331 patients. J Dermatol. 2013;40:522–527.

34) Eggleston ST, Lush LW. Understanding allergic reactions to local anesthetics. Ann Pharmacother. 1996;30:851–857.

35) Dewachter P, Mouton-Faivre C, Emala CW. Anaphylaxis and anesthesia: controversies and new insights. Anesthesiology. 2009;111:1141–1150.

36) Cohen EN, Levine DA, Colliss JE, Gunther RE. The role of pH in the development of tachyphylaxis to local anesthetic agents. Anesthesiology. 1968;29:994–1001.

37) Lirk P, Picardi S, Hollmann MW. Local anaesthetics: 10 essentials. Eur J Anaesthesiol. 2014;31:575–585.

38) Harris MH. The use of local anesthesia in the presence of inflammation. Oral Surg Oral Med Oral Pathol. 1964;18:16–23.

39) Verlinde M, Hollmann MW, Stevens MF, Hermanns H, Werdehausen R, Lirk P. Local anesthetic-induced neurotoxicity. Int J Mol Sci. 2016;17:339.

40) Auroy Y, Benhamou D, Bargues L, et al. Major complications of regional anesthesia in France: the SOS Regional Anesthesia Hotline Service. Anesthesiology. 2002;97:1274–1280.

41) Saker M, Ogle OE, Dym H. Complex exodontia and surgical management of impacted teeth. In: Fonseca R, editor. Oral and maxillofacial surgery, vol. 1. 2nd edition. Philadelphia: Elsevier; 2009.

42) Dym H, Ogle O. Atlas of minor oral surgery. Philadelphia: W.B. Saunders Company; 2001.

43) Sortino F, Pedulla E, Masoli V. The piezoelectric and rotatory osteotomy technique in impacted third molar surgery: comparison of postoperative recovery. J Oral Maxillofac Surg 2008;66:2444–8.

44) Eggers G, Klein J, Blank J, et al. Piezosurgery: an ultrasound device for cutting bone and its use and limitations in maxillofacial surgery. Br J Oral Maxillofac Surg 2004;42:451–3.

45) Misch C, Perez H. Atraumatic extractions: a biomechanical route. Dent Today 2008;27:8.

46) Sayed, N.; Bakathir, A.; Pasha, M.; Al-Sudairy, S. Complications of third molar extraction: A retrospective study from a tertiary healthcare centre in oman. Sultan Qaboos Univ. Med. J. 2019, 19, e230–e235. [PubMed].

47) Halon, A.; Donizy, P.; Dziegala,M.; Dobrakowski, R.; Simon, K. Tissue laser biostimulation promotes post-extraction neoangiogenesis in HIV-infected patients. Lasers Med. Sci. 2015, 30, 701–706. [PubMed].

48) Giorgetti, A.P.O.; César Neto, J.B.; Casati, M.Z.; Sallum, E.A.; Nociti Júnior, F.H. Cigarette smoke inhalation influences bone healing of post-extraction tooth socket: A histometric study in rats. Braz. Dent. J. 2012, 23, 228–234.

49) Ghaeminia, H.; Hoppenreijs, T.J.M.; Xi, T.; Fennis, J.P.; Maal, T.J.; Bergé, S.J.; Meijer, G.J. Postoperative socket irrigation with drinking tap water reduces the risk of inflammatory complications following surgical removal of third molars: A multicenter randomized trial. Clin. Oral Investig. 2017, 21, 71–83. [PubMed].

50) Ramos, E.; Santamaría, J.; Santamaría, G.; Barbier, L.; Arteagoitia, I. Do systemic antibiotics prevent dry socket and infection after third molar extraction? A systematic review and meta-analysis. Oral Surg. Oral Med. Oral Pathol. Oral Radiol. 2016, 122, 403–425.

51) Bortoluzzi, M.C.; Capella, D.L.; Barbieri, T.; Marchetti, S.; Dresch, C.P.; Tirello, C. Does smoking increase the incidence of postoperative complications in simple exodontia? Int. Dent. J. 2012, 62, 106–108.

52) Murph, J.T.; Jaques, S.H.; Knoell, A.N.; Archibald, G.D.; Yang, S. A retrospective study on the use of a dental dressing to reduce dry socket incidence in smokers. Gen. Dent. 2015, 63, 17–21. [PubMed].

53) Meechan, J.G.; Macgregor, I.D.M.; Rogers, S.N.; Hobson, R.S.; Bate, J.P.C.; Dennison, M. The effect of smoking on immediate post-extraction socket filling with blood and on the incidence of painful socket. Br. J. Oral Maxillofac. Surg. 1988, 26, 402–409.

54) Giorgetti, A.P.O.; César Neto, J.B.; Ruiz, K.G.S.; Casati, M.Z.; Sallum, E.A.; Nociti, F.H. Cigarette smoke inhalation modulates gene expression in sites of bone healing: A study in rats. Oral Surg. Oral Med. Oral Pathol. Oral Radiol. Endodontol. 2010, 110, 447–452.[PubMed].

55) Ozkan, A.; Bayar, G.R.; Altug, H.A.; Sencimen, M.; Dogan, N.; Gunaydin, Y. The effect of cigarette smoking on the healing of extraction sockets: An immunohistochemical study. J. Craniofac. Surg. 2014, 25, e397–e402.[PubMed].

56) Speechley, J.A. Dry socket secrets. Br. Dent. J. 2008, 205, 168.[PubMed].

57) Bacci, C. Risk of bleeding in oral surgery in patients with disorders of haemostasis. Blood Trans. 2015, 13, 176–177.

58) Svensson, R.; Hallmer, F.; Englesson, C.S.; Svensson, P.J.; Becktor, J.P. Treatment with local hemostatic agents and primary closure after tooth extraction in warfarin treated patients. Swed. Dent. J. 2013, 37, 71–77.

59) Tarakji, B.; Saleh, L.A.; Umair, A.; Azzeghaiby, S.N.; Hanouneh, S. Systemic Review of Dry Socket: Aetiology, Treatment, and Prevention. J. Clin. Diagn. Res. 2015, 9, ZE10–ZE13.

60) Bajkin, B.V.; Urosevic, I.M.; Stankov, K.M.; Petrovic, B.B.; Bajkin, I.A. Dental extractions and risk of bleeding in patients taking single and dual antiplatelet treatment. Br. J. Oral Maxillofac. Surg. 2015, 53, 39–43. [CrossRef] [PubMed].

www.ingramcontent.com/pod-product-compliance
Lightning Source LLC
LaVergne TN
LVHW061936070526
838199LV00060B/3844